GET PAID TO WRITE!

Also by Thomas A. Williams

Mallarmé and the Language of Mysticism
Eliphas Lévi: Master of the Cabala, the Tarot and the Secret Doctrines
The Bicentennial Book
We Choose America
Tales of the Tobacco Country
Poet Power: The Complete Guide to Getting Your Poetry Published
The Query Letter That Never Fails
The Self-Publisher's Handbook of Contacts and Sources
How to Make $100,000 a Year in Desktop Publishing
Publish Your Own Magazine, Guidebook, or Weekly Newspaper
What Happens When Your Book is Published (and What You Can Do About It)

GET PAID TO WRITE!

THE NO-NONSENSE GUIDE TO FREELANCE WRITING

by Thomas A. Williams, Ph.D.

SENTIENT PUBLICATIONS, LLC

Library of Congress Cataloging-in-Publication Data

Williams, Thomas A. (Thomas Andrew), 1931-
Get paid to write! : the no-nonsense guide to freelance writing /
Thomas A. Williams.— 1st ed.
      p. cm.
   ISBN 1-59181-012-4
1. Freelance journalism. 2. Journalism—Authorship. 3. Authorship.
I. Title.
PN4784.F76 W55 2003
808'.06607—dc22

                                               2003023435

SENTIENT PUBLICATIONS
A Limited Liability Company
1113 Spruce Street
Boulder, CO 80302
www.sentientpublications.com

For my uncle and head of our family,
Rupert Edward Freeman

Table of Contents

papers and magazines. Building your website. What you say on your site. Getting the money. If you build it, will they come? The secret: attract traffic with classified ads. Write articles promoting your products. Other web sales opportunities.

The rights you are selling. Check out this source of information: NWU. ASJA on electronic rights. Your compensation. By the word or by the piece. "On spec" assignments. The kill fee. Be careful what warranties you give. Copyright your work.

Capabilities brochures. Annual reports. Operations manuals. Business plans. Work with accountants. Employee manuals. Seminars. Editing and ghost writing.

Prepare a media kit. Small but powerful publications. Bombard the world with news releases. A release for every occasion. How to get on television. The payoff.

— 1 —

The Freelance Facts of Life

THE FREELANCE WRITING BUSINESS is nothing if not flexible. You can do it at home. You can do it by yourself. You can do it on weekends and evenings while you work another job. Best of all, the self-starting, reasonably creative person who will take time to learn the craft and practice it with persistence can earn a very welcome flow of extra cash.

Yes, you can do all these things, but there are some basic freelance facts of life that you are going to have to understand and live with, the most obvious one being that if you can't write you are unlikely to sell anything. Here are some of the others: ideas have to be tailored to the needs and editorial format of the magazine you want to write for; query letters have to convey certain essential information; you have to write your articles in an acceptable, lively magazine style; you have to structure your article in the more or less standard way that most magazine articles are written. The goal of *Get Paid to Write!* is to walk you through the answers to these and other questions. By the time you finish this book you will have at your disposal the tools you need to succeed. Mix in your native talent and you will be set to go. So where do we start?

What Is a Magazine?

Let's start with a crash course in the economics of periodical publishing. From the point of view of money and capital investment, just what is a magazine?

Any magazine, niche-market tabloid, or newspaper is, from a business point of view, simply a vehicle to sell advertising. If the publisher could sell the ads without the editorial support he would probably do so. That's because the publisher's profit comes from ad space sold. The purchase or subscription price a reader pays constitutes a very secondary income stream.

Any magazine that had to depend on newsstand sales or subscription income alone for its financial vitality would fold before sundown tomorrow. Remember this: no magazine with plenty of advertising has ever failed because of mediocre literary quality. Yet a magazine of the highest literary quality will be forced to close up shop in a minute if the advertising dries up. Remember *Collier's* and *The Saturday Evening Post*, and even the *Saturday Review of Literature*? They were great in their day, but are now long gone if not completely forgotten. They never lost their high literary quality, but they lost their advertising to radio and television. (Yes, there are some so-called "journals of ideas" that do not carry advertising. They also pay their writers in free copies. Have you ever tried eating a free copy?)

This brings us to fact of life number two: the amount of money that a magazine can charge for its advertising space is directly proportional to the number of readers it has. If a magazine with 100,000 readers gets $10,000 a page, then a magazine with 200,000 readers can get $20,000 a page. More readers, more money. Ever notice how difficult it is to stop receiving a magazine, even when your subscription has expired? Month after month, it shows up in your mailbox, whether you renew or not. That's because you are valuable to them even if you don't pay. They charge their advertisers for your presence on their list of subscribers. They aren't about to let you slip away from them without a struggle.

So a magazine exists to sell advertising space, period. Several things follow from this fact:

- The permanent staff of a magazine consists mostly of the business and ad sales staff.
- No magazine can afford to hire a full-time staff of writers to turn out the editorial matter that they need, issue after issue.
- Even if they could do this, the range of expertise of their staff writers would be much too limited. There's just so much any one person can know and write about.
- The editorial staff is limited to the number of editors it takes to acquire the articles necessary to make the magazine attractive to the largest possible number of readers.
- From the point of view of the business office, the job of the editor is to increase readership so that the ad sales department can increase the number of advertising pages it sells and the price it charges for that space.
- It is cheaper and more effective to buy articles from freelance writers, whose total range of expertise is virtually unlimited and who, as independent contractors, do not drag along behind them the ruinous cost of the fringe benefits which have to be paid to salaried employees.
- Editors need freelancers. They depend on them. The freelancers they do business with are their stock in trade. Editors and freelance writers are not antagonists but natural collaborators. The editor who opens your query letter is—often desperately—hoping it contains a dynamite article idea that will help attract those readers the ad people keep yelling for. If the idea is not there, it's your fault, not the editor's.

How Much Can You Make?

How much will a magazine pay you for your article? Too often the answer is "as little as it can get away with." The truth is that payment varies widely from publication to publication. Those worth writing for will pay anywhere from a few hundred dollars to two or three thousand dollars for a good, solid nonfiction article. As a rule local and regional publications pay toward the lower end of the scale and national magazines pay toward the higher end.

The Magic Circle of Success in Magazine Writing

Your targeted magazine market. This magazine buys freelance articles which will appeal to . . .

. . . businesses, which in turn will buy advertising space in your targeted magazine to reach those readers.

. . . their subscribers, people who will benefit from and can afford to buy the products and services of . . .

This diagram illustrates in graphic form the lesson I teach over and over again in this book. No matter what project you start, no matter where you start it, success depends on the completion of this circle of energy. If the positive and negative terminals of a battery are not connected, no current will flow. Similarly, if any one of these three elements is missing from your project, the process will be interrupted wherever the weak link occurs. Don't let wishful thinking mislead you. These three elements must be present for you to succeed. Nothing happens when the circle is not complete.

There are exceptions. I recently sold a short piece to *Home Office Computing* magazine and got $750 for 750 words, or $1 a word. An article for a city magazine in the Miami area brought in $1,500 for 2,500 words. The same piece in *Playboy* would have brought in $3,000 or more.

Magazines that carry a large number of less than top quality, easy-to-write articles—*Entrepreneur* comes to mind—often pay less than $1,000 for a 2,000-word article. Surprisingly enough, *Writer's Digest* and *The Writer* are also modest payers.

Many house magazines, such as *Ford Times* or the airline in-flight magazines, are top payers, and some of the most successful freelancers write for these markets as often as they can. To keep their bank accounts healthy, other writers branch out into business and technical writing where those opportunities are available. More about this in chapter 12.

Don't Give Up Your Day Job. Still . . .

So don't give up your day job just yet. The freelance trade is not a get-rich-quick scheme. But it does have its advantages. Here are some of them:

- *Chunk money.* You may not make big bucks, but what you do make you get all at one time. This is what I call "chunk money," and I dearly love it. Chunk money comes in all at once in very usable amounts. You can get a $2,000- or $3,000-a-year raise at your regular job, and it seems to evaporate before you ever get to spend it. It is spread out over so many paychecks and so much is deducted from it, it diminishes into virtual invisibility before you can buy anything with it. Not so with your freelance check. If you sell an article for $1,000, you get $1,000, and you get it now. A sum of money like that, actually and totally in hand, can put a smile on your face. You can buy something, take a vacation without maxing out your credit cards or even, perish the thought, *invest* that extra cash.

- *You can enjoy the pleasures of major tax benefits and shelters.* You don't have to own oil wells in Oklahoma or vast real estate subdivisions to cash in on generous features of the tax code. Your little home office will do much of it for you. If you use this space only for your freelance business you may be able to deduct a proportional (based on square footage) share of your rent or mortgage payment, utilities, telephone, and many other household expenses like insurance and maintenance. That can be a substantial deduction. Further, since you are a professional writer, all of the books and newspapers you buy or subscribe to become tax deductions on Schedule C (Profit or Loss from Business or Profession). Much travel also becomes deductible. I go to Chicago or L.A. every year for the four-day annual publisher's trade show, Book Expo America. It's deductible. A trip to New York for the Small Press Book Fair? Deductible. The Maui Writer's Conference? Deductible. Run all this stuff by your tax preparer or accountant as you fill out your tax return.

- *You can do it anywhere, anytime.* The third very nice thing about freelance writing is that you can do it anytime, anywhere. For all you know I could be typing this page in the sun-filled salon of my Mainship 34, anchored along the intracoastal waterway in Fort Lauderdale and cooled by ocean breezes. You can write on an airplane or in an automobile. You can do it at home, while sitting in the library, at a sidewalk café in Paris, or standing in line at the bank with notebook in hand. Anytime, anywhere at all, you can be plying your freelance trade.

- *It's good for the ego.* You become the star of cocktail parties. Everybody else just *wants* to be a published writer. You are the one who has actually done it.

The Writer's Ego: How It Helps and Hurts

Public recognition is a boon insofar as it creates an interesting, even marketable image for you as a published writer. This kind of reputation can often be turned into cash by the savvy self-promoter. But there's a downside as well. Consider these two inescapable facts about the writing business:

1. Many writers are so anxious for publication that they are willing to write for nothing, or next to nothing. This makes it harder for all of us who are trying to make a living or at least earn a good portion of our living in the business of writing. It also makes it possible for many publishers to build their businesses on the backs of writers who work for a pittance just to get recognition. The next time you hear a fellow writer say, "Sure, they don't pay much, but I'd be willing to do it for nothing," explain the writing facts of life to them and ask them if they really want to destroy what can be a very good thing for every one of us: writing well and getting paid what our writing is truly worth. This is the complete freelance circuit. Break it at any point, and the system breaks down. The energy doesn't flow. It's like an electrical circuit with one pole of the battery that powers it unattached. The energy may be there, but until the circuit is completed it's not doing anybody any good.

2. Because so many people imagine that getting published is the ultimate ego massage, everybody tries to do it. The result is an absolute storm—a deluge, a flood—of unreadable queries, unpublishable articles, unreadable stories, and abominable books swamping the offices of editors and publishers across the country all day, every day. Entire metropolitan landfills could be filled with this stuff. All this slush makes it all the harder for good writers to rise above the rabble and get noticed.

The Bad News . . .

Writers who have been freelancing for a decade or two will tell you that the magazine market has changed over the past few years, and changed for the worse. They point out that there have been many consolidations and mergers that limit market opportunities. At *Entrepreneur* magazine, for instance, one office evaluates queries for most of the other business opportunity-type magazines you see on the newsstands. Glancing at the rack, you might think that there are quite a variety of outlets for your new article on "Home Businesses You Can Start for $500 or Less." You will find that, in reality, there are far fewer than you thought. That's the bad news.

And the Good News: What You Don't See May Be Bigger Than What You See

The good news is that the market for your writing is still quite extensive. A good writer with a good idea can always sell his or her work and make money doing so. Some of the many magazine markets that freelancers often overlook are part of what I call the great, invisible market: magazines that don't normally appear on the newsstands all across the country. These include:

- Company (house) magazines (*Ford Times*)
- Trade association magazines (*Printer's Ink* magazine)
- Professional magazines (*American Dairy Farmer*)

Many beginning writers don't even know that this very extensive market exists. But it is out there, and it is big.

There are three basic resource directories that will open this market up for you.

- *Gebbie's All-In-One Directory.* Gebbie Press, P.O. Box 1000, New Paltz, NY 12561. Try their website at www.gebbie.com. Very easy to use and organized by subject matter. Published annually, a recent copy ought to be on your reference shelf.
- Though I prefer Gebbie's there are other good ones. One of these is *Gale's Directory of Periodicals.* It is fairly expensive, but

you don't have to buy it. You will find it in your library's reference room.

- The third directory you may want to use is *Working Press of the Nation,* also available in reference rooms.

First Things First Department

Most beginning writers come up with an idea first, then try to find a market for it. Pros, on the other hand, analyze the market, find out what is in greatest need, and create articles to meet that established demand. Your research and analysis of sample publications will allow you to begin to do this too, and so your well-targeted queries will become even better-targeted than before. The most successful freelance work is market driven, not idea driven.

— 2 —

How to Read a Magazine and Know What Editors Really Want

HOW CAN YOU KNOW what a magazine editor wants and needs? There's only one way. Read and study as many of his magazines as you can get your hands on, and read them cover to cover. *Really* read them. Read them analytically. Read every word on every page. Study the pictures, the cutlines, the sidebars, the graphics. Look especially at the advertising.

Check Out the Masthead

On one of the first five to ten pages of a magazine you will find a column or two listing the names of editors, the addresses of editorial offices and advertising sales offices, and other assorted information required by the Register of Copyrights and the U.S. Postal Service. The well-targeted query (see chapter 3) will be sent to one of the editors whose name appears on the masthead. A small magazine may list only one editor, so your choice in that case is easy. Most magazines, though, will list as many as five or ten editors.

Which one do you choose? The editor-in-chief and the managing editor are usually busy running the whole shebang and are not involved in the acquisitions process, though at some point they have to sign off on the contents of each issue. There will be one or more senior editors and a few plain old, unmodified editors. Choose one of these to address your query to. If the masthead lists an articles editor or nonfiction editor, then direct your query to that person.

An important note: If you use a directory such as *Writer's Market* to locate prospects, you still need to research the masthead of the current issue of your target publication. The names in *Writer's Market* will be at least a year old, and probably older, since they were gathered long before the book was printed. Further, since editors know that many beginners use this directory, the articles editor listed in its pages may be someone designated to read through the slush pile of unsolicited queries. This is definitely not where you want to be. When you get the appropriate editor's name from the masthead of a current issue of your target magazine you avoid this problem.

The masthead will also list the names and addresses of ad sales reps or offices. Write this office (you can also call) to request a media kit. Introduce yourself as representing a possible advertiser. The media kit you receive will include not only ad sales info but a complete demographic profile of the magazine's readership, editorial profiles of upcoming issues, and much more valuable information. The media kit also includes a copy of the most recent issue of the magazine.

What Kinds of Articles Does Your Target Magazine Publish?

Read every article carefully and analytically. Out of hundreds of article ideas submitted and dozens of finished articles sent in on spec, these few were chosen to be published. Your job is to think about which ones were chosen and why. What categories do these articles fit into? You will discover that there are a few basic article types. Each published article falls into at least one of these categories.

- *The how-to, or service article.* These articles are all-time winners. There are few magazines that do not use them at one time or another. If you have a fresh idea or a new slant on an old idea, you will eventually find a publisher for any well-written how-to piece. My first two published articles were both how-to's. The first one was in a magazine for public school teachers called *Teacher's Scholastic* ("How to Teach about Poetry"). The second one was an *Esquire* piece on living in France. Since then I have written and published many more service pieces. I was always on the lookout for them when I edited magazines.

How-to ideas don't have to be dramatic. They just have to be fresh and solve real problems. I once bought a regular column called "Sunday Drives" for my weekly newspaper. Each article ran to fewer than a thousand words and was accompanied by a small, cartoon-style pictographic road map. The premise was that these Sunday drives had to be short enough that the smaller children would not get cranky and start to whine before you got where you were going, and there had to be a picnic area or country store where the family could eat at bargain-basement prices. Even today, twenty-five years later, that is the one article series that I remember most fondly from those newspaper days.

You might not think that *Cosmopolitan* and *American Quilter* have anything in common, but they do. They both feature how-to's every chance they get. *American Quilter* tells you how to make the quilt and *Cosmo* tells you what to do on top of it.

- *The numbered list.* The numbered list is a subcategory of the how-to article. Readers love these articles. Short and to the point, they are very attractive to editors. They are also one of the very easiest freelance articles to write. There are no tricky transitions, no lengthy narrative threads to keep alive and kicking. I remember my earliest reading in the old and much-loved *Boys' Life*, the first magazine I ever subscribed to. I loved such one-two-three pieces as "Ten Ways to Build a Birdhouse," "How to Build Your Own Crystal Radio," "Seven Meals You Can Cook Over an Open Campfire."
- *Self-help articles.* Self-help articles tell readers how they can change their own lives for the better. These articles tell read-

A Magazine Is a Living Thing

A successful magazine is a living, organic thing, and each organ has to do its part. The editorial staff attracts readers and the marketing department sells them subscriptions. The graphic designers create a cover that they hope will stand out from all the others on the newsstand rack.

Editorial content and graphics account for roughly 40 percent of available magazine space, and sometimes less. Advertising salespeople sell the remainder of the space to vendors of goods and services who want to promote their product to the readers that the editors and subscription salespeople have attracted and retained.

The advertisers who buy the space, in turn, hire advertising agencies to design ads that will have the sell power that they need to get results. If they don't get results, they will stop buying ads and soon stop buying advertising.

If any part of this organic whole fails, then the whole of it is in jeopardy.

ers how they can make more money, be more beautiful, feel more fulfilled, develop an improved self-image, lose more weight, or enjoy more sex. It helps to enrich these articles with anecdotal success stories of persons who have succeeded in reaching the goals you recommend for others.

- *Profiles.* A profile is an article about the personality and experiences of a person of interest to the readers of a particular magazine. Some magazines carry no profiles; some seldom carry them; others carry little else. And obviously, a profile that would interest readers of *Field and Stream* would be different from one that would interest the readers of the *New Yorker*.

- *The interview.* In an interview, the same material that you might have used for a profile is presented in a question-and-answer format.

- *The round-up*. A round-up or survey article samples the opinion of experts on a question of interest. For an article called "What is the Future of ESP Research?" I contacted twenty leading parapsychologists. Round-up topics are as varied as the focus of individual magazines, the interests of readers, and the expertise of writers.

- *Nostalgia and history.* Nostalgia articles are tried-and-true pieces that tell how it was in the old days. Such articles are the stock-in-trade of many regional magazines and figure prominently in some national magazines.

- *Personal experience*. Personal experience articles relate first person adventures. These can be as varied as "How I Conquered Mount Everest" and "How I Conquered Depression."

- *Investigative articles*. Investigative articles range from governmental muckraking, to individual malfeasance, to institutional corruption. They expose the hidden truth about a subject of interest to readers. Such pieces are a venerable and important tradition in American journalism. Don't try writing one unless you are rock-solid on your facts and fully documented in your conclusions.

- *Humor articles.* Humor is a more difficult category than you might think. Timing, pace, and rhythm are everything. One man's laugh is another's yawn.
- *The essay.* The essay is the traditional "think piece." The serious ones are limited to the more intellectual, highbrow magazines, such as the *Atlantic Monthly* and the *New Yorker*. It's a tough market.

As you study your target magazines you will discover several things:

- Many article ideas fit into more than one category.
- Many of your article ideas can be varied (recycled) to fit into one or more categories, and sold more than once when completely rewritten and refocused.
- Every magazine has its favorite categories. You've got to identify these in your target publication and write your query accordingly.
- There is an editorial format in a magazine just as there is a physical format. In my own regional magazines, I always tried to have a profile, a nostalgia piece, and a personal experience/travel piece in every issue. The freelancer who noticed that would know what to send me. If you note that a magazine never uses interviews, don't query that magazine for an interview article; if you never see a nostalgia piece, don't assume that they will change their editorial format to welcome yours.

Analyze Style and Technique
Every magazine has its preferred styles and techniques. Here are some of the questions you must answer as you read through your target publication:

- Does the editor prefer a first person narrative?

- Do they prefer a lighthearted, humorous tone or an objective, impersonal one?
- Are there any special stylistic characteristics that the lead paragraphs of articles share?
- Do they prefer articles rich in anecdotes and personal experience?
- What is the average length of the articles they publish?
- Do they like lists?
- Do they like subheads?
- Do they use sidebars? If they do, your query may mention sidebar ideas.

Study the Advertising

Advertising is the life blood of any magazine. When the advertising department can sell tons of ad space, the magazine thrives. When ad sales slump, the magazine falters. Sometimes it even fails, and ceases publication.

Study the advertising that a magazine contains very carefully indeed. Ask yourself what kind of person would buy the goods and services featured in the advertising pages.

That person is your publication's target reader, the reader toward which the whole editorial content is slanted. Editors will be far more interested in article ideas likely to attract the kind of reader (the demographic base) that the advertisers are trying to reach than ones that do not.

You are wasting your time sending off-message article ideas to the wrong markets. It is obvious that you would not send an article on antique English china to *American Railroading Magazine* or an article on windsurfing to *Gum Disease Today*.

But there are more subtle differences of focus that are still very important and that will reveal themselves when you work a bit to find them. Studying the ads is a very useful way to do this.

— 3 —

The Query System, and How to Make It Work for You

A SIMPLE SYSTEM HAS developed over the years to put authors who have ideas in touch with editors who need them. It's called the query system, and it is the matchmaker of the publishing world.

A query is a letter that communicates your idea to the editor and tries to convince him that you can write an article that will be good for his magazine. If the editor reads your query and likes your idea, he may ask you to send along the finished product, either on spec (you'll be paid if the article lives up to expectations) or for a fee which he will propose in a brief freelance contract. It's that simple. First the idea. Then the query. Then the sale. One, two, three.

Write a poor query and even your best ideas don't stand a dog's chance of getting published. Write a strong query and even a mediocre idea can often find a home. Write consistently good, professional queries, and you can build a career writing articles and books. Write consistently bad, amateurish queries and the door to publication may be closed to you forever.

How to Write a Query

But how do you write an assignment-pulling query? In my years as editor and publisher of several regional magazines, I quickly became aware of three sad facts:

1. All good queries embody a common structure, yet beginning freelancers seem to be unaware of it.

2. A good query must contain nine ingredients, yet beginning freelancers continue to ignore them.

3. There are nine mistakes that you absolutely must avoid, yet writers make them over and over again.

As a publisher as well as a freelance writer, I have sat on both sides of the editorial desk. I have bought articles from writers for my own magazines, and I have sold my own articles to the editors of other magazines. When wearing my editorial hat, I found that of the thousands of queries I read, only 2 or 3 percent were well-written enough to convey to me the basic information I needed to make an informed editorial decision.

Conclusion? When you write a strong query you immediately position yourself among the *top 2 or 3 percent of all writers submitting ideas for publication.* A good query is read with interest. It inspires confidence. And it generates assignments. It does *not* do any of the things that may lead an editor to scrawl a word or two of "thanks but no thanks" in the margins, stuff it into the SASE, and return it to you.

The Terrible Ten-Second Sort

The trick is to prepare your query so that it gets the careful, thoughtful attention it deserves. You've got just about ten seconds to do this. An editor who has been at it a while can—or believes he can—tell at a glance whether the query comes from a writer capable of turning out a suitable finished product. He can tell whether the article idea is right for his magazine, and whether it meets his current needs. This instant editorial evaluation is the triage that separates letters to be read more carefully from those that will be thrown aside and returned with a "thanks but no thanks" form letter.

I found that very few queries can survive that first glance, *in spite of the fact that I wanted and needed to find a terrific idea for a maga-*

zine article in every envelope I opened. Like editors everywhere I depended on freelance submissions for material that would keep my magazines readable and interesting, build reader loyalty, and generate more newsstand sales and subscriptions. Ideas are an editor's stock in trade, and he is constantly on the lookout for them. He covets them, nurses them along, and feels an exhilaration when, in the hands of a talented writer, they develop into articles of excellence and appear in the pages of his magazine.

When an editor holds your query in his hands he will be asking himself such nonliterary questions as the following:

- Will this idea really have an impact on my readers? Will it pull its weight in creating positive reader response to my magazine?
- Will it help develop new readership? Is it the kind of article that will cause one reader to recommend the magazine to another?
- Is it short enough to fit into available space, allowing some room for graphic design? That is, is it affordable not only to purchase from the writer but to pay its way in terms of column inches in the magazine? (Long articles eat up space, and space is expensive.)
- Can I do more for my magazine by using this article than by putting some other available material in the same space?

You act very wisely when you begin to screen your own article ideas and queries with such questions in mind.

Nine Characteristics of Good Queries

There are nine steps to creating powerful query letters that, when utilized in a consistent and persistent marketing campaign, never fail to catch an editor's attention:

1. *A strong query is well-written, displaying all your skill as a writer.*

Submissions Log: Article #1		
Where Submitted	Date	Result

You can't just dash off a query. You write it with as much care as you would any piece destined for publication, perhaps even as much as you devote to writing the article itself. Remember, this is the doorway through which you enter the publishing world. If you don't write your queries carefully and well, you may never enter that door.

2. *A strong query is well-addressed (targeted).* Always address your query to an individual editor, by name. And address your query to an editor at a magazine that is likely to be interested in the subject matter you are marketing. A query for an article on child care addressed to an editor at *Popular Mechanics* is not well-addressed.

3. *A strong query contains a succinctly expressed article idea that is immediately comprehensible to the reader.* People who write sales letters and advertising copy are taught to emphasize the benefit of the product they are selling immediately and above all else. For the query-reading editor the benefit you are selling is your article idea and what it can do for his magazine. Make sure this idea is clear at the very first glance.

4. *A strong query briefly communicates the total content and slant of the proposed article, including authorities, anecdotes, and other important ingredients.* What are you going to say in this article? Your platform paragraph will do this for you (see chapter 5). Whom did you interview? Who are your authorities? What did they say? Slip in a brief, characteristic anecdote if you can. The first draft of your query may run to two or more pages as you try do all of this. Then get the fat out and reduce the query to a single page, or as close to that as you can.

5. *A strong query conveys the style and flavor of the finished product and convinces the editor that you have the skill to write the piece.* You have to sell yourself as a solid, professional writer. Take great care to perfect a query before you send it out on its rounds.

6. *A strong query tells why you have the credentials to write this particular piece.* The closing paragraph gives your credentials

and major credits. If you have any special credentials, write about them in your query. It is not so much that editors don't like newcomers to the freelance ranks. After all, everybody has to start somewhere and editors probably remember the time when they got started. But a botched, carelessly written query generally indicates a lack of skill that does not bode well for the quality of the finished product. Few time-pressured editors will want to take a chance.

7. *A strong query contains a call to action.* This can be very simple. The last line of my queries is usually "May I send (article title) to you for (name of magazine)?"

8. *A strong query is (usually) no more than one page long.* Keep it brief. Remember the words of the great French stylist Blaise Pascal, who apologized to a friend for a long letter by explaining that he did not have time to make it shorter. Take the time. Make it short.

9. *A strong query is submitted in the proper form.* Send your query on your printed letterhead, typed, with double spaces between paragraphs. The address should be typed, not handwritten, on the covering envelope. And never forget to include a self-addressed, stamped envelope.

Nine Beginner's Mistakes You Must Avoid

Inexperienced writers—most often inadvertently—stamp themselves as beginners in a number of ways. Take care to avoid all of these mistakes. While the following gaffes may seem very elementary, I have seen them all too often in the queries that I read.

1. Do not include a paragraph telling how much Aunt Minnie and Uncle Ted think of your idea and how they encouraged you to send the query in. Such familial support doesn't qualify as a part of your credentials.

2. Do not inform the editor that you are sure your article is "just what your readers have been waiting for" or that you feel

The Professional Writer

"You won't get far by . . . being timid and underestimating your abilities or worth. I meet students and new writers who say: 'I'd write a story for nothing in order to get into print!' That, and any notion remotely akin to it, is the attitude of an amateur, and editors, though often willing to gamble on a new writer, are never drawn to amateurism. The professional writer is not one to stand around humbly, like a beggar at the back door. He tries to offer something good, and in a manner that suggests self-confidence, and self-esteem."

—Hayes Jacobs, in *Writing and Selling Non-Fiction*

certain that "everyone will be excited by it." You may feel this way, but leave such judgments up to the editor.

3. Do not include anything in your query that hints you are afraid someone will "steal your idea."

4. Submit absolutely nothing in longhand. No one will take the time to read what you have written.

5. Don't specify what payment you wish to receive. When an editor accepts your work he will tell you what his rates are. At that time you can accept them, reject them, or negotiate them.

6. Don't forget the SASE.

7. Unless there is a good reason for doing so (a time-sensitive subject, for instance) don't give an editor a deadline for replying. Write a follow-up letter if there is a long delay in getting a response. Meanwhile circulate your query to the next name on your list.

8. Don't submit your query on fancy, colored paper. It's white bond and white bond only.

9. Don't submit your query on paper of non-standard size. Stick to 8.5-by-11.

Why Many Editors Steer Clear of Beginners

Even though you are an amateur at the business of writing for money, it is important not to advertise this fact. That is the purpose of avoiding the beginner's mistakes I just listed.

Many editors avoid beginners at all costs. Here's why:

- Beginners are often not capable of converting an idea into a publishable article. Their ambition outstretches their ability. They are like carpenters who show up on the job site full of spit and vinegar, but who are unable to make a square corner or saw a straight line. There is a craft to the business of writing. It can be learned, but you have to take the time to do it. Even a beginner with a very good idea is not likely to produce a publishable article without considerable editorial input.

- Beginners often resent an editor's efforts to rework their material to make it publishable. The attitude "I'm an artist. I wrote it like that, and that's the way I want it" is all too common among amateurs.
- For reasons that I have never understood, beginners are frequently afraid someone is going to "steal" their ideas, so they set up all kinds of barriers to keep what they imagine to be unscrupulous and avaricious editors from doing this. The truth is that the idea is just the beginning. It's the conversion of the idea into a professionally written article that counts, and that is what only you, as a writer, can do. For more on this topic, see chapter 9.
- Beginners often do not study their target magazines to understand the style and format that the magazine prefers.

Exceptions to the Rule

Fortunately, exceptions to the no-beginner rule are sometimes made, and as a newcomer to the freelance trade you will keep trying until you luck up on one. To illustrate, I will quote a letter I received from Bill Ryan, then an editor at *Esquire*. I was a beginner, but Bill Ryan liked my article idea ("A Year in France on $1,000") enough to give me a shot at writing it. He wrote:

> The piece can be improved, I believe, and by a few more facts: Where are the French universities? What kinds of towns and areas? How do you look for a room in a French town? There is some repetition that might be trimmed too, I think. Good work. I hope you will want to make these few alterations and return it to me. If it clears Don's desk as it did Tom's and mine it should be good for about nine months in France.

How to Get Productive Again

Writer's block got you down? I suffered an acute case for many years. As a writer I was my own worst enemy. Then I read Dorothea Brande, where I found this simple bit of advice. "Act as though it were impossible to fail," Dorothea advised. For years, like some malevolently negative parrot perched on my own shoulder, I constantly fed messages into my ear. "You call that writing?" I would say to myself. Or, "That's the sorriest stuff I ever saw." Or, "Nobody in his right mind would call that poetry." Naturally, this didn't help at all. I then began to play Dorothea Brande's game. I didn't have to believe it, I simply had to *act as though I believed it.* I began to write as though it were impossible not to write good, strong lines. And you know what? I began to write more of them than I had ever been able to do before.

You got that? Only 1 percent of on-spec submissions by beginning freelancers ever get to first base at *Esquire* (admittedly a very tough market to crack). For that reason neither Bill Ryan nor other *Esquire* editors could afford to spend a great deal of time trying to develop them. I was very, very lucky. Ryan made an exception in my case and took a chance on me, even though I had never published an article in a major magazine before.

If your idea is a strong one, and if you are persistent and consistent in the submission of your queries, you will ultimately find an editor willing to take a chance on you. Every article you sell eases the way to the next sale. I enclosed a clip of the *Esquire* piece with all future queries. I'm still doing it to this day when I submit queries to new markets .

You may find an editor of a lesser magazine who is willing to work with beginners and help them structure their articles. At my regional magazine, our writer's fees were on the low end of the acceptable pay scale, so I tried to give writers a bit more than just a check; I wanted to give them a chance to learn, and to do so I was always willing to go the extra mile.

Why Good Queries Are Rejected

Sometimes even good queries are rejected. This is usually due to one of the following reasons:

- An editor has bought everything he needs for the foreseeable future and is simply not interested in buying anything else.
- His magazine published an article on a similar topic in the recent past and he doesn't want to repeat himself.
- Your idea is not right for the magazine. Either the subject matter is wrong or the article type is wrong or the style is wrong.

You can't do anything about the first two reasons for rejection, but you can definitely do something about the third one with a little research and a lot of attentive reading.

— 4 —

Ideas and How to Get Them

WHERE DO IDEAS COME from, and how do you get them? These are the favorite, sometimes desperate questions of writers who come to my seminars on the freelance writing business. They complain that when they sit down to write or when they think about writing it is as though their minds go blank and they become complete, unimaginative dunces. I can remember a time when I felt much the same way. Now my only problem is finding the time to write about all the ideas that I am constantly conjuring up or simply deciding which of them to write about next.

What did I learn that made so much difference? There were just a few essential insights, simple and profound at the same time. In this chapter I will tell you what they were and how you can use them to get your own idea-producing juices flowing.

The human brain—yours included—is, of and by itself, a twenty-four-hour-a-day, non-stop idea factory. That's its nature. Don't believe it? Well, you dream don't you? And your dreams combine the wildest, most powerful and emotion-laden images and events imaginable. Who created those dream images and those events? You did; no one else. And there's a lot more where that came from. The creative flow is always there. You've just got to learn to access it (and harness it) while you are awake. How? Here are some things I've learned about getting ideas.

A Good Idea Is Worth Its Weight in Gold

Good ideas are like gold. None of us has so many of them that

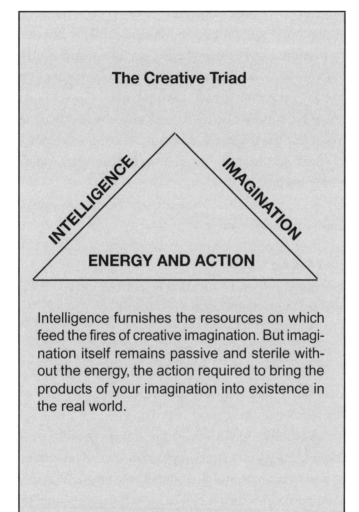

The Creative Triad

Intelligence furnishes the resources on which feed the fires of creative imagination. But imagination itself remains passive and sterile without the energy, the action required to bring the products of your imagination into existence in the real world.

we can afford to throw them away. And yet that is what most of us do, day after day, if we are not careful to prevent it. The fact is, our minds are constantly generating and emitting ideas. But many of us spend a lifetime not honoring our own ideas and not paying attention to them. We force them back into the shadows of our minds where they lie dormant or simply disappear.

The more we ignore our own creativity, the less accessible it becomes to us. But the reverse is also true. The more we pay attention to our ideas and take the trouble to capture them, the more numerous they become.

So why don't we do this? Here are some of the reasons. Most of us will easily recognize them.

We Just Don't Believe It

Much of our childhood education is spent squeezing the imagination out of us. It prepares us, at best, for the SAT exams that we take as high school seniors to get into college. Unfortunately, these multiple choice obstacle courses only measure the facts we have in our heads. The SAT has a section on verbal skills and a section on mathematical skills. It has no section on creative skills and so does not measure what we imagine. Imagination is the great creative force. It tells us what to do with those facts. It was a fact that steam, like other expanding gasses, exerted pressure on the vessel that contained it. It was imagination that invented the steam engine.

A young person is truly lucky to have had one single teacher who understood and taught his students about the power and value of imagination. Men and women who accomplish things are those who combine a native intelligence with imagination and—the third side of this creative triad—energy. For writers that means having brains enough to write in the first place, imagination to figure out what to write about, and the energy to do the actual writing once we get around to it.

We Are Our Own Worst Critics

So, for whatever reason, we don't value our own ideas. We admire the ideas of others but think of our own as having little or no worth. If you have even a hint of this way of thinking inside you, think again. We are all human beings; we all share the same life experiences; we are all caught up in the mystery of what life is about. Are there strange beings in outer space? You bet. It's us. We are as strange as they come. How could such strange, mysterious, complex beings not have imagination? Open yourself up; let it all flow out. Respect your own mind. After all, it really is a miracle.

The Idea Vanishes before We Capture It

Our ideas will disappear on us if we are not careful to capture them. To understand just how evanescent an idea is, imagine this: You are in the wilderness, trying to start a fire with no matches. You strike a piece of flint with a metal bar. Sparks are emitted, but the life of these sparks is the merest fraction of a second. They are gone almost as fast as they appear. But catch one of them in a small pile of tinder, and it will ignite, creating a tiny flame that you can then use to start your campfire, warm your hands, cook your dinner, keep wild animals at bay—whatever you want.

Ideas are like those sparks. They come to us when our minds are struck by some event, some conversation, or even by some other idea. Like those sparks, they are here one minute and gone the next, unless you take care to preserve them.

To do this, keep a small pocket notebook and immediately jot down ideas as they occur to you. Don't evaluate your ideas or insights. Just jot them down. If other thoughts and elaborations on this idea occur to you while you are writing, jot them down too. These first, spontaneous idea associations are often very valuable. Later you can read through your notebooks and see what is useful and what is not.

I have stacks of such notebooks on my shelves. When I leaf back through them I am often amazed at the rich source material I find there—material that I had completely forgotten about. I call this process of idea capture and preservation "mind harvesting." It is essential to you. It is not so much how to get ideas but how to preserve those you do get.

The Importance of Specialization

Successful freelancers develop one or more areas of specialization. My own specialties include education (I am a former college professor), writing (I have written twelve books) and publishing (I own book and magazine publishing businesses). To these I have added an adjunct specialty that is much in demand these days: the ins-and-outs of running a home-based business ("world headquarters" of my book publishing business, Williams & Company, is a remodeled bedroom in my Georgia home).

Specialization has great advantages:

- It focuses attention and primes the idea pump. After you live with your specialties a while, you will begin to notice all those things in your environment that relate to them, from newspaper articles, to comments on television shows, to casual conversations. The business of a writer, said W. H. Auden, is "to notice things." Specialization lets you know what you are supposed to notice and sharpens your attention so that you recognize it when you see it.
- Your own interests and personal experiences enliven what you write and make it more immediate to the reader.
- You gradually build a reputation as an expert in your field. Editors and readers begin to recognize and trust your name when it appears as a byline. Eventually, editors may begin contacting you to assign an article in the area of your expertise. When this starts to happen you're in high freelance cotton.

The Relationship of What You Are Writing about to What You Know

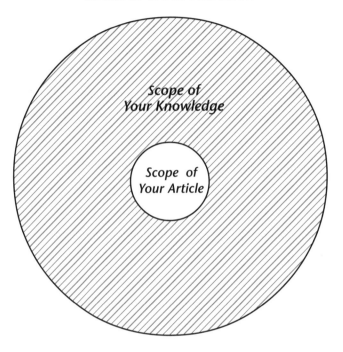

The shaded area represents the extent of your knowledge of your subject. The smaller, white area represents what you are using of your knowledge. The greater the scope of your knowledge is relative to the scope of the article you are writing, the more solid and authoritative your work becomes. Readers can easily sense whether or not you have the expertise you claim to have.

- You build a body of knowledge that becomes a very valuable stock in trade. Whatever your subject, you need to know far more about it than the part you are writing about. Such broad knowledge gives a depth to your articles that would not be present without it. The graphic on the previous page illustrates this point.

Mind-Mapping

I first encountered this technique in a book by Tony Buzan called *Use Both Sides of Your Brain*. It may have been around before, but that's where I found it. At one of my seminars I met the father of a thirteen-year-old girl who, inspired by Buzan, wrote a little book called *Mind-Mapping for Kids,* which she packaged as a method for getting term-paper ideas when you don't think you have any. The last time I checked, she had sold a total of 10,000 copies in the United States and Australia.

Though some people dismiss mind-mapping as a simplistic tool suitable only for amateurs, I have found that it works very well for me as a powerful idea generator. This very book was mind-mapped before I started to organize and write it. The technique is based on the indisputable fact that though we claim to think abstractly we really use free association and images to organize our ideas. We draw pictures in our minds.

Mind-mapping (it could just as easily be called idea-mapping) is easy to do, though you have to do it right. It works through idea association and is done almost automatically. Your critical intelligence—the part of the brain that often sits around telling you how dumb you are—is put on temporary hold.

Here's what you do:

1. Sit down at a table with a legal pad and a pencil.
2. Draw a circle in the middle of the page. In that circle write the word or phrase that describes the idea you are working on or want to work on.

3. Let your mind roam free. When some related idea occurs to you, draw a line from the original circle to another circle and put the new idea inside. When another idea occurs to you, draw a line from the main circle or the secondary circle and form a new circle, in which you put the new idea.

4. Continue in this way as fast as you can. Don't evaluate as you go. Don't stop to think. Don't draw perfect circles. Don't check spelling. Neatness does not count. Don't worry about drawing straight lines. Just write. After a couple of trials you will have it down pat.

Sound simple? It is, but it works. By way of illustration, I've included a copy of the basic mind map I drew when planning a section in chapter 5 of this book, "The Freelancer's Paradigm."

Basic Human Needs and Desires

Use the basic desires and drives that all humans share to develop ideas. Examples of these are the desire for *sexual fulfillment*, the desire for *increased wealth*, the desire for *personal beauty*, the desire for *personal fulfillment*, and the desire for *enhanced self-worth*.

You generate article ideas by linking a subject matter area to each of these drives. Let's try this with an idea about the "amazing power of the mind" and see what we come up with. We'll link it with each of five basic needs.

- Sex: "The Psychology of the Orgasm: Mind Games and Sex Games"
- Money: "Mind and Money—The Hidden Connections"
- Beauty: "Beautiful Mind, Beautiful Body"; "Think Young, Be Young"
- Personal Fulfillment: "The Imagery of Self-Fulfillment"; "Peace of Mind and How to Get It"
- Self-Worth: "Your Hidden Mind Power"; "Personal Power through Mind Power"

A Sample Mind-Map

On the following page I have reproduced the actual mind-map I used to develop ideas for for the "freelancer's paradigm" section in chapter 5. I scratched it out on a legal-sized yellow pad. Note that neatness does not count in mind-mapping; you are writing as fast as you can with no self-critical brakes on your imagination. My handwriting is not the clearest in the world even when I am trying, so here is a little help.

The circle in the middle has the words "freelancer's paradigm" in it. The vertical line to the top of the map ends with a circle called "craft and art." To the left is a note: "[The paradigm is] like an optical illusion. It suddenly clicks into place, and you wonder why you haven't seen it all along." To the right is a circle called "variations." Feeding off of this are the letters a, b, and c, to remind me to show variations. Continuing clockwise is the word "Examples." Feeding off of this are the initials TW (for examples from my own articles), "news," "movies" and "great how-to books." Following this you see "examples from business writing," "from the general to the particular," "The human interest element," "use of anecdote," and, further along, "my experience as an editor."

By the time I had finished this mind-map, I had topics for the entire chapter spread out before me.

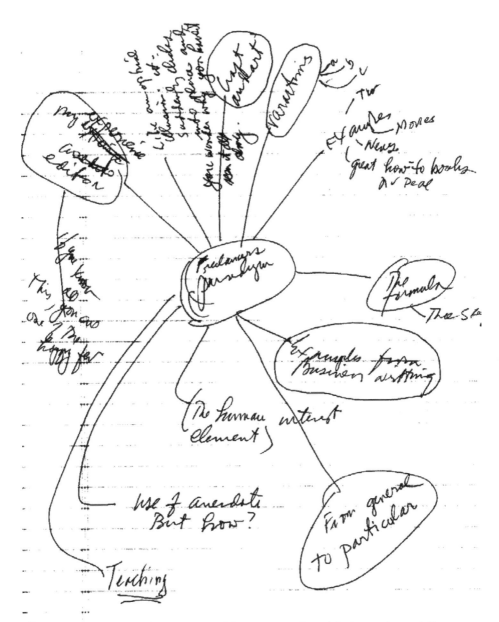

By following the guide on page 39, you may be able to make out the meaning of some of these mind-map scribbles. I show this page from my notebook to underline the fact that in making a mind map, you write swiftly, and don't stop for self-criticism, fine penmanship or anything else. Note, too, that wherever possible, I use abbreviation and brief notes to remind me of my idea rather than taking the time to note it down in its entirety.

After this exercise, we could mind-map any one of these ideas to see how we might refine and develop it.

I see some potential in two of them which seem to connect to my own background and interests: "Peace of Mind" and "Think Young; Be Young." Both could be fairly easily done with a lead, a list, and a close, taking care to match the slant of the articles to the editorial needs of particular target magazines.

Read, Clip, and File

I've said that you've got to notice things. One place to notice them is in every magazine or newspaper you read, for whatever reason. The questions "Can I use this?" and "Is there an idea here for me?" should always be in the front of your mind.

1. Read the *New York Times* and other major newspapers every Sunday. Don't stop reading until you find one or two ideas you can use.
2. Read books and magazines that contain information relevant to your specialty. Copy or clip the articles that fit the bill.
3. File these away in your idea file.
4. When the file folder gets too fat, subdivide the files. Winnow them every month or two and throw out dated or dead material. At the same time, read through them and remind yourself how smart you were to have clipped them in the first place.

It's Time to Take Action

Have you ever wondered why the names of the same writers seem to appear in local and regional anthologies, magazines, and small press reviews over and over again; why the same people are always appointed to arts commissions, asked to give talks and write introductions, participate in arts festival programs, get appointed to state arts posts, and lead seminars at yearly writers' group meetings? It's not a matter of luck, nor is it a plot that these names appear so frequently on "noted writer" lists. It's just that these people have managed, one way or another, to create a public visibility adequate to build a literary reputation. When organizers or grant-givers fish around for the name of a writer for some purpose or other, they naturally choose from those that they have heard about. Don't waste time complaining about this; accept it. It is simply the nature of the world.

Why, you ask, do they keep overlooking *me?* If you have heard that still, small voice of longing to be better known murmuring deep within you, you are not alone.

If you want to become a part of this higher echelon, you must let people know who and what you are. There is no ostentation here, no unjustified self-aggrandizement. It is just a matter of taking the simple and gentle steps that will ensure your success as a writer.

— 5 —

The Professional Writer's Toolkit

Who can confidently say what ignites a certain combination of words, causing them to explode in the mind? Who knows why certain notes in music are capable of stirring the listener deeply, though the same notes, slightly rearranged, are impotent. These are high mysteries

—E.B. White

EDITING A MAGAZINE IS often a frustrating experience. So when my editorial eye fell on the rare piece of writing that had that powerful, indefinable something that made it perfect for my publication, the effect was almost electric—especially after I had spent the morning wading through a slush pile of other submissions that did not have it at all.

Stylistically perfect pieces have everything going for them: rhythm, tone, just-right illustration and anecdote, perfectly tuned quotes, and the most supple and fluid transitions possible. There is nothing to do to such pieces except pay for them and run them.

Anyone who has an aptitude for writing possesses to one degree or another some talents that can't be learned or taught: an ear for the sound and music of words, a sense of the rhythm of language, and a facility of expression that makes it easy for others to understand what they are saying.

If you don't have these qualities—not even a hint of them—no one can give them to you, and you probably ought to take up some other trade. You can't teach a tone-deaf person to play the violin. In the same way, you can't teach a person with no feel for language to

52

hear the difference between a good sentence and a bad one. That's the bad news. The good news is that if you *do* have some small reservoir of talent hidden away inside, you can get better and better at using it. Here's how.

How Did He Do That?

The first step is to look at the work of other writers you admire and ask yourself, "How did he do that?" or "Why is reading this article so much easier and so much more fun than reading that one?" Then look at your own writing and ask, "Where did I go wrong with this line?" or "Why doesn't this anecdote work?" "What did that writer do that I can do?" When you ask these kinds of analytical questions you are getting into the heart of what the tools of the trade—the stylistic basics—actually are, and you will get some pointers on how to use the most basic of them—the writer's equivalent of the carpenter's hammer, pliers, screwdriver, and saw.

A Personal Example

I remember telling a friend many years ago that I wanted to make my living with "words and books." For the most part, I have succeeded in doing that, but it has not always been easy. Judging from letters and other things I wrote when I was very young, I have always had a natural feeling for words and how to use them, but I have not always been a good, professional writer.

Like many a young person interested in writing, I went to college and took a literary major, then went on to become a professor of comparative literature. I very soon discovered that the "publish or perish" stories I had heard were all too true, and I began writing the kind of scholarly articles that get published in professional journals. I was pretty good at this, and so I climbed the academic ladder without great difficulty.

There came a time, though, when I became more interested in the writing than in the scholarship. Style is not a big deal in academic circles; if fact, if you write too well and too readably, you may even be looked on with suspicion by journal editors. You are too "popular" in tone and not "scholarly" enough. That is why the great thinker William James has never gotten his due as psychologist or philosopher. His writing is beautifully luminous and clear.

I wanted to try my hand at writing for magazines, and to do this I knew that there were a great many academic kinks I had to get out of my style. I studied the work of writers I wanted to sound like, and I studied the scholarly essays I had written up to that time. I came up with some clear distinctions. Here are just a few: Scholarly writing (including my own) was as impersonal as one could make it; magazine writing was, whenever possible, quite personal. Scholarly writing (including my own) feigned "scientific" objectivity; magazine writing was enlivened by the idiosyncratic views of the writer and of those whom he interviewed and quoted. Scholarly writing (including my own) was hog-tied by authorities and convention; the best magazine writing was as free as the wind.

Little by little I managed to free myself of these habits and restraints. One of the hardest stylistic flaws to overcome was a peculiar kind of backwards sentence structure favored by the scholars. I had to trade this in for a more direct way of expressing myself. For example:

Backward: *Making a living as a freelance writer is hard to do.*
Direct: *It is hard to make a living as a freelance writer.*

Backward: *What was foremost in my mind was the fact that I*
needed the money.
Direct: *The fact that I needed the money was foremost in my mind.*

The Six Most Common Flaws, and How to Remedy Them
A full treatise on style is far beyond the scope of this book, but this chapter points you to six of the most common—and easily re-

paired—stylistic flaws that I used to see in articles that less-experienced freelancers submitted to me. Many an otherwise good piece was returned to its author because of them. I did not have time to repair these flaws myself and I did not have time to teach the writer how to do it himself. Here is my list of the basic six.

1. Poor Structure: The Anatomy of a Magazine Article

The great majority of freelance nonfiction articles that are published share a common structure. You can vary it and add your own spin, tone, and style to it. But the structure is there nonetheless. If you want to succeed you've got to understand and master it.

Here's an analogy. We humans, though we are all different, share the same physical characteristics. The structure of our bodies is the same—head at the top, neck, torso, legs—right on down to the feet. Put the head on the end of an arm and you don't have a person, you have a mess.

Get the structure of your article wrong, and you also have a mess. Here are the article parts you've got to recognize and use.

- *The Title*. A good, strong title helps sell an article, and you owe it to your editor to do your best to come up with one. A good title can make a lot of difference in the reception your query gets. Without it a query might not get read at all. I once sent out queries for a book called *How to Make Money in Local and Regional Publishing*. I got no takers. I sent out the same query with the title *How to Make $100,000 a Year in Desktop Publishing* and almost immediately got four publishers who wanted to see sample chapters. One of them, Betterway Publications, offered me a contract within a couple of weeks.
- *The Lead*. The lead paragraph has two jobs to do. The first job is to get you to read the next paragraph, whose purpose is to get you to read the next one, and so on through the article until you come to the end. The second job is to establish the tone of the article: Is it humorous? Matter-of-fact? How-to?

First person experience? Intellectual? When you look at the leads in a given magazine you can discover a lot about the tone the editors like and slant your lead to satisfy those likes. The same article can be written with different leads to appeal to different editorial needs. The lead for my *Esquire* article on living in France was right for that magazine:

> Don't look now, but that bible of budget travelers, Arthur Frommer's *Europe on Five Dollars a Day* isn't feeling well. It's down with acute inflation. The first symptom was a discreet little chapter at the back of the last year's printing about the very real possibility of spending just a little more than the basic five. From there the trouble spread to the title itself. The new edition has dropped all pretense. It's called Europe on Ten Dollars a Day. So when I invite you to consider an entire year in France on $1,000, I can see you reaching for the granum salis you doubtless carry in your handy pocket pouch. Especially when reading travel articles.

This lead would have been different had I written the article for *Mademoiselle* or *Working Woman*—no "handy pocket pouch," for one thing. But the body of the article would have been substantially the same. If you come up with a really solid lead you can put it at the top of your query. I did this with the following lead, written for a piece I published in *Home Office Computing*. The editor who read it responded that she was "intrigued by my lead" and wanted to see the rest of the piece. It went on to be published. Here is that lead:

> When I stepped out of the elevator into my lawyer's 10th floor office I knew I was in trouble. A half acre of lush carpet stretched before me with a receptionist's desk looming in the distance and half

the skyline of downtown Charlotte, NC, visible through the vast, tinted glass wall behind her. I could already feel the tug on my wallet before I began to spell out my legal difficulties. And I was right. Though my case was settled out of court I received a bill for $5,007.56—$5,000 for legal services and $7.56 for copies made on his office machine, at .25 each. He wasn't missing a bet.

The whole feel of the article is there: hapless entrepreneur at the mercy of big-time lawyers. It is also clear that I am going to treat the subject with at least a measure of humor and that everything I will say is based on dire personal experience.

- *The Platform or Billboard Paragraph.* The billboard paragraph follows the lead. This paragraph tells the reader what is to come in the rest of the article and prepares him to read through it. Here's the platform paragraph from that *Home Office Computing* article:

  Now, I'm not here to bad-mouth legal counsel; we all need it from time to time. But I did vow that the next time I set out from Williams & Co., Publishers (the 150 square feet of my den devoted to my home-based business) to visit an attorney, I'd be prepared to minimize the number of billable minutes relentlessly ticking off on his desktop clock. I worked out then and there seven ways to slash my legal bills.

- *The Body of the Article.* In the body of the article you deliver what you've promised in the platform, being careful to preserve the tone and style of the opening paragraphs. In the lawyer article I go on to tell about my seven rules of action.

In the *Esquire* article I tell precisely how to spend a year in France on $1,000: do this, then this, be careful of this, and be sure to do this. The body of the article is the easiest part, but you have to know what you are talking about, and talk about it in a lively, readable style.

- *The Close.* The close doesn't have to be dramatic, just a little tag to let your reader know that you're done with him. The close to my article on lawyers was simple and to the point, but it did its job:

> As long as I'm in business, I know I'll need expert legal advice. But now I know the costs and, more important, how to control them.

This analysis may seem simple, and that's because magazine articles have a quite simple structure. But simple or not, you'd better adopt it if you want editors to buy your work.

2. Inappropriate Tone

Every magazine strives to maintain an editorial feel—a tone — that it considers right for its readership. It is a little hard to define tone, but everyone knows what it is. You could say that tone is the flavor of a magazine: comic/humorous (*The Onion*); yuppie (*Gentlemen's Quarterly*); scientific/abstract (*Scientific American*); down-home (*Mother Earth News*); sophisticated (*The New Yorker*); nothing-but-business (*Wall Street Journal*); highbrow (*Atlantic Monthly*).

You need to study your target magazine both for writing your query and, when you get a positive response, for writing your article. My query to *Esquire* some years ago for the article called "A Year in France on $1,000" brought a note of interest from a senior editor who offered to read an "on spec" submission largely because

I had scrapped my non-targeted, all-purpose lead for one appropriate to the tone of that particular magazine. I must have gotten the tone right, because *Esquire* bought the article. Looking back at it, I think I did capture the yuppie tone favored by the magazine. Its readers were predominantly college grads; they were men; they saw themselves as world-travelers-to-be; they were flattered by my use of the common Latin phrase *granum salis*; and most of them knew, at least by reputation, Frommer's book.

3. Omission of the Telling Detail

The telling detail gives density and believability to any article and helps maintain focus and tone. Compare these two sentences:

> I walked up the stairs and knocked at the door.

> I walked up the stairs and knocked at the sagging door. Someone had recently painted it a lugubrious gray. Abandoned bristles from a cheap paint brush were encrusted in the finish.

The first version presents bland, generic stairs and generic door, communicating nothing at all. The second gives details that characterize the entire ambiance of the action.

You don't need much, just a stroke here and a stroke there. In this way you incorporate into your writing the little things that reveal personality and truth. Without the wrinkled trench coat and last-legs Peugeot, the character we are watching on TV would be just another detective. With them we are watching a richly characterized investigator named Columbo. The details do the trick.

It is the specific word that fleshes out the detail of a narrative, not the general, undifferentiated one. Just a moment ago, I reached down into the wicker magazine rack beside my chair and pulled out the first magazine on the stack, *Southern Lady*. I flipped it open at

Freelancer's Hierarchy of Style and Craft

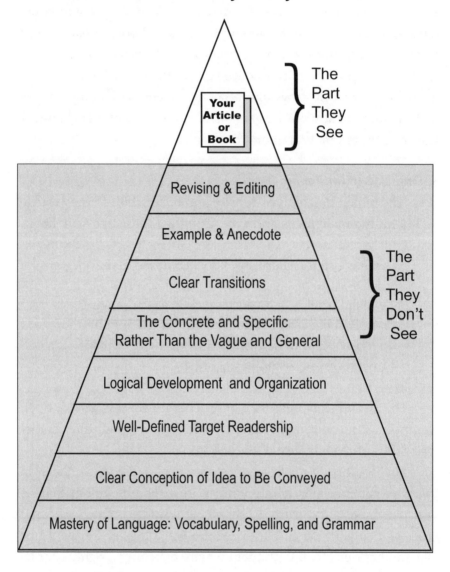

Your
Article
or
Book

} The
Part
They
See

Revising & Editing

Example & Anecdote

Clear Transitions

} The
Part
They
Don't
See

The Concrete and Specific
Rather Than the Vague and General

Logical Development and Organization

Well-Defined Target Readership

Clear Conception of Idea to Be Conveyed

Mastery of Language: Vocabulary, Spelling, and Grammar

Successful freelancers bring a full bag of tools and skills to every job of writing. The better they write, the more nearly invisible these tools are. The skills lie below the surface and provide the foundation that supports the whole edifice.

random and found an article telling the story of Lori Taylor, founder of TaylorG women's clothing. Author Phyllis Hoffman tells us how Lori, having completed her first designs, "waltzed into the showroom of her first apparel market with six garments in hand." A writer given to the general might have said she "entered the showroom" or "presented her garments in the showroom." Instead, Phyllis Hoffman uses the more specific expression "waltzed," conveying both the atmosphere of the occasion and the personality of Lori Taylor. And she waltzed in not with some garments, mind you, not a few garments, or a variety of garments. She did it with six— count them, six—garments.

This is the kind of detail I look for as an editor and work hard to include in my own writing. The lesson here: *Look for and communicate the telling detail, and in doing so always prefer the specific word to the abstract or general word.*

4. Awkward Handling of Quotes

Quotes are the lifeblood of most nonfiction writing, yet are very often misused or clumsily used. I will go into more detail on quotes in a later section of the "freelancer's paradigm." For the moment, though, let me make a few basic observations.

When it comes time to insert a quote, many beginning freelancers seem to throw up their hands and get the dirty work done any way they can. A dead giveaway of quote-handling trouble is the use of the words "states" or "stated" as substitutes for "says" or "said." I can't explain the fondness for this stilted phrasing, but when I meet it early on in a piece, I know that I am reading the work of a fairly inexperienced writer. I am not surprised to find other traces of break-in status as I read on.

The fact is that people, in general, do not *state* things, they *say* things. How many times have you said something like, "I saw Tom yesterday, and he stated that he was going on vacation." I'll wager that you have never said it. What you do say is that you saw Tom and he *said* he was going on vacation.

In a police report, people state things, and when the President asserts this or that to be true, he may state things. But ordinarily we simply say things.

So we will avoid the "stated" trap at all costs. We will also vary the way we structure our quotes. There are three ways to introduce them into your narrative: the up-front "said," the tail-end "said," and "said" in the middle.

Take the sentence: Tarzan said, "My best friend is a hairy ape." In this example the "said" is up front.

In the sentence, "My best friend is a hairy ape," said Tarzan, the "said" is of the tail-end variety. But one can also say it this way: "My best friend," said Tarzan, "is a hairy ape." This is the "said in the middle" version.

These three arrangements allow for variety and also for characterization. Another technique that allows for characterization is the use of modifiers to give more specific meaning to the general word. "My best friend," said Tarzan coming to a sudden realization of his good fortune, "is a hairy ape." One can also substitute another word entirely for *said*. "My best friend," bragged Tarzan, "is a hairy ape," or "My best friend," Tarzan lamented, "is a hairy ape." This can be an effective tool, but should not be overused.

5. Transition Trouble

Transitions relate the parts of your article to one another just as the joints of our extremities propel our bodies along in the direction we want to go. Without the joints, the arms and legs don't work, and the body goes nowhere.

Transitions do the same thing for your writing. With strong transitions, your article is a functioning, organic whole, delightful to read and easy to understand. Without them, your article consists of disjointed clumps of written matter, which, at best, drag themselves painfully along from beginning to middle to end—if any reader is willing to stick with you that far.

The word "also," stuck alone at the beginning of a paragraph, is a common first symptom of transition trouble. It is usually stuck there doing duty for some other word that ought to be there but is not. Like the word "stated," the up-front "also" is a dead giveaway that the writer who put it there has not learned how to use transitions.

The job of transitions is to relate each paragraph or thought to the next one in a logical, immediately understandable way—explicit or implied. Explicit transitions consist of words and phrases like *in addition, moreover, therefore, for example, meanwhile, on the other hand, in the last analysis,* and a great many others. Though the meanings of some of these words are similar, most are not interchangeable. Think carefully and write carefully when choosing one of them.

Other transitions are less explicit. The lead sentence of a paragraph can indicate in a number of ways its relation to the paragraph that preceded it. In a book about the publishing business, I wrote:

> One of the great problems in publishing a weekly newspaper is the scheduling of time. Ad sales, editorial deadlines, layout, printing—all this has to be done on time, day after day, week after week. You can't let anything slip and still get a newspaper out on time. When I was editor of the *Mecklenburg Gazette,* I . . .

And I go on to tell how I encountered and overcame the problem of schedule slippage. "When I was editor of the *Mecklenburg Gazette,* . . ." is the transitional phrase that lets the reader know an example illustrating the previous statement is coming his way. With this transitional sentence in place, the more explicit "for example" is not necessary.

I will mention two other widely used freelance techniques for creating transitions. The first is that of the transitional question. In the above example on newspaper scheduling, my second paragraph might have begun, "How did I handle it?" using a question to direct the reader's attention where I wanted it to go. One sees the transitional question often, even though it is not as elegant as some other techniques.

A second transitional technique, and one favored by many editors, is the use of subheads within the text of the article. Subheads lead the reader along, molding his expectation for the next idea that is coming his way. Subheads also serve to break solid columns of text in a way that makes them seem less daunting and more readable. Whichever technique you choose, the transition must be there, and it must work.

6. Lack of Anecdote and Illustration: The Freelancer's Paradigm

For many years I published regional magazines and weekly newspapers. To help beginning writers whip their material into shape for these traditional break-in markets, I explained to them that anecdotes and personal experiences were the lifeblood of readable articles. I put the basic structure of good nonfiction writing into "one, two, three" form and gave it a name: the freelancer's paradigm. Results were almost immediate. Marginal articles, rewritten with this guideline in mind, suddenly became publishable articles.

The Paradigm Is a Pattern

The paradigm is a simple pattern, but very important pattern. It works the way our minds work, moving effortlessly from the general to the particular, leading the reader on with effective storytelling. This pattern consists of three parts:

1. A general observation, statement of fact, or question;
2. Followed by a narrowing of focus to a single case;
3. Followed by an example, anecdote, or quote.

The following paradigm comes from the lead paragraph of the same *Southern Lady* article we looked at earlier. Note its very clear construction:

> You can usually spot a TaylorG garment. It's a combination of wonderful fabrics, so creatively detailed with buttons, ribbons, and trims, the outfit instantly snatches your attention. "Women want to feel special, and my garments make them look pretty," says Lori Taylor, who founded TaylorG in Dallas, Texas, 11 years ago.

In this paragraph, freelancer Phyllis Hoffman has used the technique of the paradigm: general observation (*You can spot . . .*), a narrowing of focus (*combination of wonderful fabrics, etc.*) and a quote (*"Women want to feel special . . ."*). Nothing dramatic here, just good, solid magazine writing. The better and more experienced the writer, the more invisible and seamless the paradigm becomes. In the hands of a seasoned pro, it is open to virtually infinite variation. But whatever form it takes, it is always there.

The Paradigm Is Basic

The freelancer's paradigm is basic to successful magazine writing. The magazine nonfiction article is a highly compressed form: in the space of 1,500 to 2,500 words the writer must hook the reader, lead him through the article easily and enjoyably, and teach him something useful, all served up with a liberal helping of human interest. The paradigm enables the writer to do this. It is an antidote to the stale air of abstract fact. It lets the fresh air of personal, one-on-one experience waft through your narrative.

In an article for *Publishing for Entrepreneurs* magazine, I wanted to get across the idea that anyone with imagination and energy can make money publishing advertising-based local and regional publications. I could have started my article in a very matter-of-factly:

Periodical publishing on the local and regional level can be quite lucrative. Publishers of tabloids, city magazines, and tourism guides regularly make incomes of $100,000 a year and more. Today the typesetting and page layout capabilities of desktop publishing have put such projects within the reach of any entrepreneur who will take the trouble to learn to use them. Statistics reveal . . .

Instead, I opted for the paradigm:

Hometown publishing is a low-cost, high-payoff opportunity. I went into this business five years ago with a Mac Plus, two used desks, and a laser writer. This year my company will gross $800,000. Next year we expect to top $1,000,000. What I did, you can do too.

General observation, particular example, and personal experience. This paradigm-based lead not only tells the story, but whets the reader's appetite for the details to come. The facts are there in both versions, but the paradigm translates them into the language of personal experience and makes them come alive. (The paradigm, by the way, can make a strong lead for a query. It tells an editor a great deal about your slant, your wit, and your writing style.)

Here's another paradigm from the same article (note the question used as transition):

Can anyone succeed? Yes, if you have the energy and ambition to do so. "I never believed I could bring out my own newspaper, " says Harold Hall, of Richmond, Virginia, proud publisher of a new weekly. "Your book gave me the details, and look at me now!"

The paradigm is not flashy or dramatic, but it works. After my article was published, visits to my website (mentioned in a tag at

The Paradigm and the Nightly News

The paradigm is everywhere. Because it is a mode of communication that is basic to all effective transmission of ideas, you find it in spoken as well as written media. The nightly news could not survive without the paradigm, which moves effortlessly from the general observations of the news anchor to the particular and then to the inevitable sound bite of the individual reporter in place. "Nature is a powerful adversary," Peter Jennings intones from his New York studio. "When disasters strike no one can withstand them. The people of Argus, Oklahoma, learned this firsthand this afternoon as a devastating tornado ripped through the town. John Johnson has the details." Jennings then asks "John, what are things like in Argus tonight?"

Reporter Johnson appears on the screen, standing before a wrecked mobile home park. "Peter, the people here are just trying to assess the damage and begin to pick up the pieces."

He turns to a distraught woman standing beside him. "Mrs. Wiggs, you have lived right here for five years. Now your home is gone. What will you do?"

"We'll just have to go on living the best way we can," Mrs. Wiggs replies bravely. "That's all we can do." Again, the paradigm moves from the general (nature's power) to the flesh and blood particulars of Mrs. Wiggs's cabbage patch, and ends with a quote. And it works, every time.

the end of the article) zoomed and sales of my book on periodical publishing peaked at a level five times greater than before.

Here's another paradigm, this time from my book, *Poet Power: The Complete Guide to Getting Your Poetry Published* (Sentient Publications):

> If you want to publish your poetry, remember that opportunity doesn't do the knocking, you do. In his classic manual, *Think and Grow Rich*, Napoleon Hill tells how he got the job he set his mind on. "I applied in the regular way," Hill recalls. "I didn't get hired. I then sent a follow-up. I did this every week for four weeks. When that failed I sent a letter every day. Finally I sent a telegram every hour for two days. At the end of this time I got a call. 'Come on in to work,' the voice said. 'We give up. The job is yours.'"

And I concluded:

> While I do not recommend this degree of overkill in approaching editors who will not have the time to deal with all these inquiries, it is essential to develop a marketing plan appropriate to your goal of getting your poetry published and implement it relentlessly.

Some very successful books are almost entirely constructed of paradigms. This is particularly true of the classic bestsellers of salesmanship and motivation. *Think and Grow Rich*, Zig Ziglar's *See You at the Top*, W. Clement Stone's *Success Through a Positive Mental Attitude*, and Dale Carnegie's *How to Win Friends and Influence People* all fit into this category. So do more recent titles such as Wayne Dyer's *Your Erroneous Zones*, and on a somewhat more intellectual level, M. Scott Peck's *The Road Less Traveled*. Not to mention the granddaddy of them all, Norman Vincent Peales's *The Power of Positive Thinking*.

Here's what you, as a writer, need to remember about such books:

- They communicate easily and directly. (Do you?)
- They are paradigm-based, putting their lessons into easy-to-remember paradigm form. (Is your own work paradigm-based?)
- They are all-time bestsellers. (Why not join the crowd?)

Everybody Uses the Paradigm, Even the Highbrows

The paradigm appears in the most unlikely places, and even the most highbrow authors ignore it at their peril. Take the case of Immanuel Kant and René Descartes. Kant wrote a monumental tome called *Critique of Pure Reason*. Descartes wrote a slim volume called *Discourse on Method*. Both writers were brilliant. Both altered the course of the history of ideas. Yet only one of them—Descartes—is widely read, widely quoted, and universally hailed today as the "father of modern philosophy."

Why is this so? It is the power of the paradigm. Kant's book is a dense and virtually impenetrable jungle of thought, a veritable collapsed universe of ideas and analysis. Descartes, on the other hand, starts out with a first person narrative and a fabulous use of the paradigm (paraphrased here).

"I always wondered," Descartes begins, "why mathematicians agreed on everything but philosophers agree on nothing, "Then one cold winter—it was 1637, I believe—I was holed up in a small room, stoking a potbellied stove and trying to keep warm, and I had an idea. What philosophers needed, I decided, was an absolutely universal starting place, a proposition like 'a straight line is the shortest distance between any two points,' But was there any such proposition? I proceeded to doubt every idea in my mind, except for one. I could not doubt that I was doubting. My thought processes prove at least my own existence."

"I think," Descartes concluded, "therefore I am."

This is not just great philosophy, it is also a perfect paradigm.

The Greatest Teachers

The greatest teachers use the paradigm naturally. We think of the lessons of the Bible, for instance, not as theological propositions but as stories illustrating universal truths. "What is wisdom?" the writer asks, and follows up the question with the story of King Solomon, the two mothers, and the child.

"Where did death and suffering come from?" the Old Testament asks. Well, it seems that in the beginning there was a beautiful garden, and a tree which bore forbidden fruit. . . .

"What is the sum of all philosophy?" the Buddhist prince asked the greatest scholars in his kingdom. They thought and thought, and came up with many long answers, but the prince was not satisfied. "Distill your answer to its essence," he demanded. The great scholars finally came up with an answer. The sum of all philosophy, they told the prince lay in a simple affirmation: "This, too, shall pass."

In every case it is not the idea that the reader remembers, but the flesh and blood story. And embedded in that story is the point that the writer wanted to get across. That's why the freelancer's paradigm is the first and most basic tool of all nonfiction writing.

— 6 —

Eight Success Secrets of the Masters

SUCCESSFUL PRACTITIONERS OF THE freelance trade—the ones who get published regularly and make significant amounts of money— share certain characteristics and abilities. They approach their work in an organized, systematic way that gets results. What works for them will work for you. If you've got the ability to be a writer in the first place, you will learn what the masters do and then do the same things yourself.

1. The Masters Specialize

The masters develop specialities which allow them to focus on a limited number of subject matter areas. This, in turn, allows them to develop real expertise, establish a reputation for themselves in the publishing world, and get assignments. I discussed specialization in chapter 3.

Then, after working in specialized fields for a year or two, the freelance masters gather the pieces that they have done, add to them, and publish a book. A published book among your credits adds considerable weight to any query letter.

2. The Masters Recycle

The masters recycle good ideas, formatting and slanting them for different markets. They get top mileage out of each and every idea. Suppose you had some expertise in home schooling. You could do a straightforward how-to piece (where to get books, how to get

71

accreditation, how to get through a year's work in a year's time). Then you could write a piece on the religious dimension of home schooling, another on the socialization problems (for the child) that home schooling can pose, even a *National Enquirer*-style exposé (I Was Homeschooled—and I've Got the Bruises to Prove It!).

3. The Masters Write Every Day

So you don't feel like writing today. So what? You may not feel like writing tomorrow either. But if you want to make money writing, if you want to learn to write better, if you want to learn to write faster, you will do it anyway. Wherever their work is, everybody goes to work, every day. That's what sets the professionals apart from the wannabees of the world.

Writing is hard work. So is bricklaying. But the bricklayer gets up every morning and reports to the job site. Too many no-shows and he gets fired. It's simple. Bricklaying is his job. He lays brick or he doesn't eat. That's the way buildings get built. Writing is your job. You've chosen it. You do it every day, just like any other job. Like it or not, you do it. That's the way articles get written.

4. The Masters Revise What They Write

Professionals understand that writing and revising are two entirely different brain functions. When you write, you let it flow. Write first; revise later. Remember, you can't create and criticize simultaneously. First one, then the other. When the time comes to revise, play with what you first wrote. Move stuff around. Polish the transitions. Find the right word. Smooth out the rhythms. Develop the lead.

For me, revision works best when I do one thing at a time. Here's how I do it:

1. I read through the whole article (or chapter), eliminating repetition, fleshing out my narrative, adding ideas and ex-

amples that occur to me as I read through. (It was during revision that I added the analogy of the hose to the section on writer's block in this chapter.)

2. I read through again to check on logical development, moving paragraphs and entire sections around as needed.
3. I read through to find anything in the article that will make a strong lead or a strong title.
4. I read aloud for rhythm and smooth out any awkward sentences.
5. I proofread to correct spelling and grammatical errors. The spellcheck on your computer is useful but not sufficient. It is not context sensitive and can't tell the difference between "their" and "there" or "it's" and "its."
6. Then I put the piece aside for a day or two and read it again later.

5. The Masters Observe the Rule of One

Editors don't make or break a career. Writers do this for themselves. One person is responsible for your success or failure in freelancing, and that one person is you. This is the *Rule of One*.

6. The Masters Observe the Rule of Twenty-Four

When you have worked up an article idea and written a query, write the names of six periodicals that might be interested in it on your query submissions log (see page 21). Send your query to the first three publications on the list, taking care to slant it to the editorial needs of each publication. When a thanks-but-no-thanks response comes back to you (and many surely will), immediately send a query to the next publication on your list and add a new publication to the bottom of your list. This way you always have three live queries out for each article idea, and you always have three magazines in line to submit to. Here's the kicker: You send a new query out no more than twenty-four hours after you receive a rejection. This is the *Rule of Twenty-Four*, and it can work magic.

On Action and Impulse

When I notice that assignments are drying up and the checks don't seem to be coming in as regularly as I would like, it is a sure sign that I have been a little lazy—slow to develop ideas and slack in sending out queries.

In this business you've got to be persistent and consistent. There's no substitute for working every day at your trade. I don't mean dreaming about it or even thinking about it. I mean actually *doing* something about it.

I also notice that I haven't been following up on ideas and impulses that pop into my mind. Some of my most important sales have come as a result of acting on an impulse. I was finishing up a manuscript on a book called *How to Publish Your Poetry*, when it suddenly occurred to me that I ought to send a galley to the Writer's Digest Book Club. I didn't really think about and didn't expect anything to come of it. I had never contacted a book club before. Nevertheless, I stuffed a galley (produced on my laser printer) into an envelope and sent it off. A few weeks later, I got a call from the book club. They wanted it and purchased 1,500 copies.

Follow your impulses. It doesn't cost a thing and can pay off in a big way.

7. The Masters Observe the Rule of Seven

When you receive a positive reply to a query, followed by a contract for your article, finish a first draft within seven days. *Mark your calendar and do it.*

If you have received no positive replies during any seven-day period, review your idea file, firm up a new article, and write a new query.

These two things constitute the *Rule of Seven.*

8. The Masters Overcome "Writer's Block"

We go for coffee between paragraphs. We put off writing the next sentence. We stare at the computer screen and stall rather than get started.

Why? There are many reasons why we put off writing, and all of them are bad. In my own case I used to freeze (and still do, sometimes) because I am secretly afraid that the next bit I write will not be as good as I want it to be, and I think a lot of writers share that debilitating self-doubt. Some of the greatest writers of our time have shared it. So what else is new? You will write the best you can, no better and no worse, so get at it.

Remember the writer's golden rule: *You can't create and criticize simultaneously.* If you get it backward and act as your own worst critic before you even get started, the gears seize up and the creative motor grinds to a halt. If, while doing a first draft, your critical self keeps looking over your shoulder at the screen of your computer and telling you that you are writing garbage or haven't got it right, you are acting as your own worst enemy.

Here's an analogy. You are watering the lawn or washing the car. The water comes out of the hose in a useless dribble. You look back and see a kink where the hose has doubled up on itself. You shake the kink out and the water flows freely. You've got all of it you need. It was there all the time.

Your creative mind is like that hose. Self-criticism is the kink. There is plenty of creative juice there but it's not flowing through your fingers and onto the keyboard. So shake the kink out; scrap the critical attitude. Just let it flow. Just start writing. There's plenty of time for the critical part when you begin the process of revision.

For me, putting self-criticism on a back burner is a miracle cure. It will be for you, too, if you get it right. I just plow ahead as though it were impossible to fail. I write some of my best stuff this way.

— 7 —

How to Write for Newspapers and Syndicate Your Own Column

NEWSPAPERS ARE OF INTEREST to freelance writers in three ways: as an unpaid, break-in market for book reviews, op-ed pieces, and similar, portfolio-building clips; the opportunity for an occasional assignment for a feature article or two; and a home for the regular publication of your own column. Of these three, only one is likely to produce meaningful income: that self-syndicated column.

Chaos Is Real and Time Is Short

If you have never worked for a newspaper or visited the newsroom, you can't imagine the deadline pressure that accompanies the production of every single issue. Somehow, in spite of everything, it all comes together by press time, even though the whole project seems threatened by near chaos until moments before the presses start rolling.

This is true for weeklies as much as for dailies—perhaps even more so, since the weeklies may have only two or three people to get the whole job done, including layout and delivery. This means there is no time to coddle or even edit outside writers. So if you do get a newspaper assignment, write carefully, observe the word-count limit scrupulously, and, if you ever want to work for that publication again, get your piece in on time.

Newspapers do have staff writers. The number of them varies

widely. The small weeklies get by with one or two, including the editor, while the *New York Times* has a high-rise building full of them. Further, they have many sources outside the newsroom for materials that they publish. The news-feature syndicates furnish full-length feature articles on everything from arts and entertainment, to sports, to world events backgrounders. These come complete with professional photography, sidebars, graphs, maps, and other art. Though some of the largest dailies have staff writers or stringers in most major capitals, national and world news is usually furnished by wire services like the Associated Press. This includes news of all kinds. Only the local news is written in most newspaper newsrooms, only local sports stories are written in the sports department, only local business in the business section, and so on.

Nevertheless, the pressure to get a paper out every day or every week means that editors will, from time to time, buy features and columns they need but have no one on staff with the time or the expertise to write.

The opportunities for freelancers are slim, but they do exist. If you are just breaking in you can try your hand at writing op-ed essays for the editorial page or an occasional book review, but these are usually unpaid contributions. At most, the papers provide you with a free book—the one you reviewed—and tear sheets to add to your portfolio. Such tear sheets can be useful to the start-up freelancer, but there comes a time when you have more than enough of them and want to move beyond the freebies to more profitable ventures.

The Big Dailies

Some of the larger dailies do assign occasional articles to freelancers in specialized sections—lifestyle, the arts, travel, etc. — and these do pay. When I was living in South Florida a short while ago, the *Miami Herald* was paying $250 for such pieces. But this happened on relatively rare occasions, and the writers who got the jobs were well-known to the assigning editor. Newspaper people are simply too rushed to work with writers whose skills and experience are not familiar to them.

Though a check for a couple of hundred dollars can be welcome from time to time, the fee is certainly at the very low end of what you need to earn to make a viable writing career—even a part-time one.

Niche-Market Tabloids

There are other newspaper writing opportunities more akin to the magazine market, except that they also pay less. These consist of the many special-interest, niche-market tabloids that are published, usually weekly, in many cities. The bigger the city the more of these tabs there are. They are almost always free-circulation publications.

The niche market tabs range in slant from the laid-back to the sensational. Savannah, Georgia, where I currently live, is a relatively small city whose greater metropolitan area counts 230,000 inhabitants. In Savannah there are four niche-market tabloids: *Coastal Senior, Coastal Arts and Antiques, The Business Report and Journal*, and *Connect Savannah*. The first three of these are pretty well defined by their names; the last strives toward an arts-alternative niche. All accept queries from freelancers. The going rate of pay seems to be close to $100, give or take $25.

Nobody is going to get rich writing for such markets, but an occasional byline gives the writer local visibility that he may parlay into other, more profitable assignments. In addition, these publications are open to freelancers who are euphemistically referred to as "emerging writers," that is, so-far unpublished ones. The competition for a byline is less fierce than that encountered when you query publications of national circulation. In larger metropolitan areas the money will be better, but it will be harder to break in.

To Pitch an Idea

Newspapers and special-interest tabloids constitute a different kind of market. Everything is speeded up. Decisions are made quickly and publication can occur within days of acceptance. To pitch an article idea, call the target editor and ask how he prefers to get queries, via email, fax, or regular mail. Those I deal with prefer email these days, but I understand that some do not. A telephone call also gives the editor an opportunity to let you know if he does not want to look at queries.

The Real Opportunity: Syndicate Your Own Column

By far the most lucrative and interesting way to make money writing for newspapers is to write and sell your own, self-syndicated column. Every newspaper needs and uses columns to attract and serve their demographic base. Editors know that readers develop column loyalty. They know where their favorite column will appear and often turn to it first when they unfold their paper.

Columns begin small, but, with luck and persistence, can finish very big indeed. The "Dear Abby" column began with one newspaper. It was gradually syndicated to a thousand or more and ended by making a fortune for writer Abigail Van Buren. Dave Barry's humor column, initially published only in the *Miami Herald*, went into national syndication and made Barry a nationally famous—and prosperous—writer.

Such people are the stars of the business. But there is a lot of room for writers of less glittering reputations to earn sizeable incomes with their columns. Thirty-nine-year-old Jim Miller of Norman, Oklahoma, came up with an idea for a question and answer column called "The Savvy Senior." Miller says he started "The Savvy Senior" for fun, but soon discovered that a great many readers liked what he had to say. "It's amazing how many seniors are isolated and don't know where to turn for help," Miller says. "A lot of stuff we take for granted can be very complicated for older people.

There's so much information out there for them to deal with." Miller first published his column in the *Norman Transcript* as an unpaid contributor. In short order he had expanded his column to 400 papers, each of which paid him $3 to $5 a week. ("Three dollars a week is quite a bit of money for a lot of small papers," Miller says.) But even at those modest prices he earned an income of $40,000 a year.

Profile of a Column

A successful column is a tightly written piece that contains as many of the elements that will make any article as readable as possible: a direct, personal tone; anecdote and illustration; quotes. It will be very short—50 to 700 words. Yet within this limit it must have a beginning, a middle, and an end, satisfying the reader that you have fully dealt with the subject at hand.

The ability to write such precise, lean prose is the *sine qua non* of the aspiring columnist. If you haven't written for newspapers before, you'll be surprised how few words it takes to fill up fifteen or twenty column inches on a page of newsprint.

A strong, memorable title will help your column achieve the visibility you are working for. The newspaper environment is cluttered with news stories, features, cartoons—even crossword puzzles. You want to rise to a spot as near the top of the heap as possible. You can scarcely overestimate the importance of the name you give to your column, so spend the time it takes to find one that really works. When you've found it, you will know. Don't settle for next best.

Your title should immediately identify the subject matter and do it in a memorable way. "The Savvy Senior" is such a title. It is brief and to-the-point. The use of the slang "savvy" and the alliteration of the two-initial "S" sounds, and the rhythm of the two short, two syllable words help make it work. Combine as many of these characteristics as you can into your own title. You want an editor's attention and interest to be piqued at first glance.

What a Column Does

A successful column deals with a topic of interest to the greatest number of people in the broadest possible across-the-board category ("Dear Abby") or to virtually everyone in a niche-market category ("The Savvy Senior"). It tells readers how to solve problems or achieve goals that are very important to them. Jim Miller's "The Savvy Senior" is a such a column. Below is a list of some other popular categories for service columns. I jotted these down literally as fast as they came to mind:

- Personal finance: earning money at home, coupon clipping, job hunting, minding your money, etc.
- Health and fitness: weight loss, diet, holistic healing, health tips.
- Personal relations: social life, love life, advice, family, child care.
- Self-Improvement: do you make these mistakes; vocabulary building; self-education.
- Arts and entertainment: book reviews, restaurant reviews, travel tips, etc.

There is no end to solid column ideas. But remember that it is your unique slant, the contribution that you, personally, bring to your piece, that will make it saleable and readable and that will build a loyal following—and thereby please your editor mightily.

Profile of a Columnist

So that's what makes a column. Now, what about the columnist?

- A newspaper columnist is a solid, dependable writer. When an editor buys a column, he expects it to be ready to print. He is not interested in editing it. There must be no false notes, no kinks, no typos, no stumbles, no errors of any kind.

- A newspaper columnist writes on schedule and misses no deadlines. The editor who has bought your column expects to have it in hand, on time, for every issue. No one will have time to contact you or encourage you. You produce or you don't. "Unreliable columnist"—the very phrase is a contradiction in terms. As a syndicated columnist you want to be the one writer the editor doesn't have to worry about.

- As the author of regular, running commentary on a single topic, a newspaper columnist is extremely well-informed on that topic. If you are going to write about earning money at home, you need to know more about the subject than you could use in a year's worth of columns, and you need to be learning more all the time.

How Much Do You Earn?

The are two ways to make money: get large amounts of cash from one source—one of Stephen King's three book deals, for instance—or small amounts from lots of sources. The newspaper columnist falls into the second category, charging newspapers $5 and up for one-time use of each column.

What a newspaper pays for a column is often linked to circulation. Weekly newspapers, which are likely to be among the first purchasers of your work, often have circulations of as few as 1,000 subscribers. My own weekly, the *Mecklenburg Gazette*, had a circulation of 4,000 when I sold it, and it was quite successful.

If you set your rates according to circulation, you will have to set some minimum for your column. A $5 fee could cover the first 5,000 in circulation, with an additional $.50 per thousand added on for additional thousands. There will also be a maximum. Ten dollars will be about as much as you can expect to get, the very outside of what any paper will be willing to pay.

You will be competing with material furnished in large quantities by the national syndicates, such as the New York Times Syndicate, the Christian Science Monitor Syndicate, King Features Syndicate, Tribune Media Services, L.A. Times Syndicate and others. These syndicates sell their columns to small papers at rates close to what you will be charging. The payoff is in the numbers. There will be a considerable up-front investment in time as you write columns and sell them to the first three or four papers to order them—a lot of work for $20 to $30 a week. But if you continue to market your piece, and if it is good, you will gradually add subscribers. Even fifty subscribers at $5 each will give you a monthly revenue of slightly over $1,000. This is not bad for four short, 700-word pieces. As the number of subscribers grows, so does the income earned by those same four columns.

Marketing Your Column

Once you have chosen your topic and written ten or more sample columns, you are ready to begin the process of self-syndication. Syndication, by the way, is simply the process of offering the same column to various, non-competing newspapers that do not share the same readership in a single trade area. If there is a weekly newspaper in a town, for instance, as well as a special-interest tabloid, you do not sell your column to both of them.

Create a Sales Package

The first step is to put together the following materials for your sales and promotion package:

- Tear sheets of any columns that may already have been published. Often writers have contributed freebie columns to local newspapers or tabloids for some time before beginning to explore the idea of self-syndication. If you have done so, and the columns are examples of your best work, make copies of tear sheets to include with your syndication package. You can also include copies of other articles that help establish your expertise in the area you are writing about, especially if you do not have any published columns.

- Copies of at least five new, unpublished columns. This provides an interested editor with a month's worth of material (yes, some months do have five publication days) and eases his mind about long-range continuity. Editors want to be sure that you have the ability and energy to turn out columns on schedule. Announcing a new feature that appears for a week or two and then mysteriously disappears is a no-no in the newspaper business.

- A promo sheet for yourself as author. Your promo sheet should be as powerful as you can make it. Pretend that you are spending several thousand dollars to place the flyer as a display ad in the largest, most expensive (in terms of the cost of ad space) daily in your state. Work on it just as hard as you would on that four-figure advertisement. The promo sheet should contain:

1. A photo of yourself. The photo should be a mug shot, but not one of those posed ones that the studios turn out for your mother's mantelpiece. Instead, shoot it informally in your place of work, with some relevant scenery in the background. Spend some time getting it right. Later, when you place your column with a paper, you can write a news release announcing the new feature and send the photo along with it.

2. Information about you and your credentials. Why are you writing this column? What qualifies you to do so? Where and how did you acquire your expertise? Omit anything not directly related to the job at hand—selling your column. You may be president of the PTA, but unless your column deals with the problems of public schools, this fact is irrelevant.

3. Relevant journalistic credits.

4. Testimonials, feedback, quotes that highlight your ex-

pert knowledge of the subject matter you are dealing with. The promo sheet should be written in easy-to-read, clear-at-a-glance format. In this and all other copy, use a bulleted or numbered format whenever possible.

- A flyer for the column itself: Again, work as though you are spending thousands of dollars for a premium ad position in a metropolitan daily. That is to say, sweat the details. If the flyer doesn't do its job, it will cost you thousands of dollars by burning prospects who might otherwise subscribe to your syndication. Here's what your flyer should contain:

  1. Technical details. Column title, length, how your column is delivered (email, fax, snail mail), and a contact name to get questions answered.
  2. Full information on your column. What is your target readership? What topics will you cover? What questions will you answer? This should be written in an easy-to-read, clear-at-a-glance format.
  3. Testimonials, reviews, reader comments and blurbs praising your column or your writing in the field.
  4. Cost and special offers. Special offers might include the first two (or more) columns free, discount for quarterly payment, three-month trial offer at half price, etc. If one offer is not pulling positive response to your satisfaction try another on the next fifty packages you send out. Test the market in every way you can.
  5. A postpaid reply card. The card works better than a postpaid reply envelope because it is quicker and easier to handle. The target editor just checks the appropriate box and throws it into the "out" basket. The card itself must be the essence of clarity. Here's what goes on it:

     - Acceptance of the offer
     - Terms

- Rights
- Choice of mode of delivery (if there is a choice)
- Signature

Assemble Your Package

When you have designed these materials, print enough of them to see you through several hundred submissions.

Print a brief cover letter on your letterhead. This will presumably be on a higher grade stock, but the other materials in your promo package can be printed on simple 60 lb. offset (20 lb. bond). Mingle colored paper with white to make your package more interesting.

Your reply card and some of your other items can be printed in two colors. This need not cost any more than a single color. Some of the small, franchised print shops have a "free second color day." On those days you can get a second color for the same price as a single color. Minuteman printers, which I sometimes use, offers such a special. However, paid or free, the second color is worth the money.

Collate the materials and stuff them into catalog envelopes. You can buy these wholesale in white and other colors from suppliers who deal with local print shops. Two such suppliers that I have dealt with are Mac Paper and Arvey's. When mailing time comes, use attractive labels with your return address printed on them. If you do not wish to order these from Nebs or some other vendor of office supplies, you can make your own, wholly acceptable ones with a package of Avery labels, your color printer, and a simple layout program.

Plan Your Marketing Campaign

Marketing your column will require a substantial investment of time. It is not likely that dozens of newspapers will immediately subscribe to your syndication, but the long-range payoff can be attractive, both in terms of regular, monthly cash flow and in terms of secondary profit centers (see below) as well.

Your first job will be to assemble a prospect list of a hundred or so newspapers that you plan to contact. Your prospect data bank will include the editor's name, since your package should always be addressed to the individual who can make a decision. Smaller newspapers—especially weeklies—will generally have a single person running things, while larger papers will have individual editors for the various sections: sports, lifestyle, arts, etc. You will add to this name the street address, email address, telephone number, and fax number.

There are several standard sources for compiling such information, most of which you will find in the reference room of your library. Always be sure to use the latest edition for your research so that the information you gather will be up-to-date:

- *Gail Directory of Publications*
- *Editor and Publisher International Yearbook*
- *All-In-One Media Directory from Gebbie Press*

Enter the addresses into your computer using a program that will prepare address labels. You can buy these at Office Depot or comparable stores for $20 to $30. You don't need anything too sophisticated. Something simple like the "My Mailing Label" software will do. Some word processing programs, such as Microsoft Word, also have a feature for preparing labels.

Market in Concentric Circles

At the center of your newspaper-columnist world are the newspapers and tabloids in your immediate trade area—your home city or county. Try hard to place your column in one of these publications. If you have to give someone a free trial of three months or even six months, do so. The important thing is to get into print, attract some reader attention and reaction, and accumulate some clips to reproduce in your marketing package.

Since these publications are nearby, you can make some personal sales calls to help break through editorial resistance to any new feature. Remember that you must convince the editor that your column is a strong, reader-pulling feature, that you are good enough as a writer to pull it off, and that you will not call in sick—or the equivalent—when the time comes to take your kids to Disney World.

From that beginning, reach out in ever-expanding circles to nearby towns and counties, to your state, region, and, ultimately, the country as a whole.

An Example

My friend Ron Gallo, a park ranger and fishing guide in Fort Lauderdale, has written a series of books on bass fishing. Three years ago he began to write a fishing column for a regional edition of the *Miami Herald*. For two years he wrote his column—dubbed "Neighborhood Angler"—gratis. The public visibility it brought for him and for his fishing guide business was return enough on his investment of time.

In the last year the *Herald* has begun to pay him the same fees as they pay any other regionally published columnist, that is to say, very little. Nevertheless, Ron is now a paid columnist and has clips and reader comments to add to his syndication package, not to mention strong praise from his *Herald* editor.

Recently, he has placed his column with two non-competing publications in the South Florida area and is ready to send subscription packages to Florida newspapers. He will target the southeastern states next and then go national.

Ron Gallo has a very good chance of achieving his goal to become a widely and profitably syndicated columnist. He is an expert, and his column is full of the kind of information that outdoor buffs love. The "expanding circle" method he is using to market his column is the one I recommend to you.

Sending Out the Package

Put your cover letter, promo sheets, and tear sheets into a catalog envelope, cover letter on top, new columns on the bottom. Print your return address on this envelope, along with some promotional copy.

Take some time to design an envelope that is attractive as possible. Think of it as a book cover that has to look better and more tempting than any of the others on the bookstore shelf. Use a colored ink that will show up well against the white background.

The promo copy can be something like, "Dr. Tom Williams's great new column on making money at home" and even include a blurb: "Tom Williams's column helped me earn an extra $1,000 a month in my own home!" Or perhaps a promotional message, such as "First month free."

As you begin your campaign, here are some things to remember:

- Most weekly newspapers are published on Tuesday or Wednesday, so that the ads they contain will be in circulation before shopping starts in grocery stores and malls on Thursday, Friday, and Saturday. This means that Monday, and especially Tuesday, are very busy times. If you have never seen a minuscule weekly newspaper staff struggle to get the paper to press on time, you don't know the meaning of the phrase "working under pressure." Time your mailings so that your syndication package does not arrive in the midst of this weekly chaos.
- Follow up in a week's time by email, fax, or telephone. Make it easy for your prospect to get back in touch with you.
- Re-mail your package to the same prospects at least twice within the first few weeks, and every quarter thereafter.
- Vary your approach and your special offers to see what works best, then settle down and stick with it.

Secondary Profit Centers

The money you make writing your column is not the only way

you will benefit from your syndication. If you have a book in print, the tag at the end of your column ("Tom Williams is . . .") will lead readers to it and thereby increase sales. If you do not have a book out there, your column can help you get one. Publishers prefer writers with personal visibility and whose name is known to large numbers of readers.

In addition, once you are established, you can give seminars and talks, and write other articles on the subject of your expertise for magazines and the Internet.

Why Not Start Your Own Newspaper?
It's Easier Than You Think

Weekly newspapers and specialty tabloids are very attractive entrepreneurial projects, and well within the reach of the two-person publishing company. Such publications have a lot going for them and are easier to get going than you might think. These publications also meet our criteria for success: they have a clearly defined and limited trade area, and target a finite list of advertising prospects, all of whom are easily reached. Moreover, tabloids are inexpensive to design and produce.

There may be some modest start-up costs, mainly for office space and initial supplies. (You can avoid the space cost if you have a large enough basement or double garage that could be converted into an office.) Most equipment, chiefly your computer, laser printer and enlarging/reducing copy machine, can be leased. Production tables, files, and other paraphernalia are generally very simple to design and can be homemade.

These virtually negligible upfront costs are more than balanced by the short weekly billing cycle you will be working on. By the time your next month's lease payments come due you will already have four or five (yes, some months will have five Wednesdays in them!) weeks' accounts receivable to pay them. If, in the beginning, you do not need to draw out great amounts of cash for your own living expenses, it really is quite possible to start a newspaper and pay for it out of current revenues.

This is precisely what I did with the *Mecklenburg Gazette*, a weekly newspaper that I owned in Davidson, North Carolina. When I got hold of it, the newspaper was literally a week away from bankruptcy. I had no cash to speak of—just a few thousand dollars in savings to live on until advertising revenues started coming in.

People with shared interests, ethnic and religious groups, and for university towns, incoming students (Student's Survival Guide to . . .) are just a few examples of the population segments that could form the base of a profitable publication.

If this idea interests you, consult another title in the Sentient Publications Culture Tools series, *Publish Your Own Magazine, Guidebook, or Weekly Newspaper,* also by Dr. Tom Williams.

— 8 —

Need an Agent? Here's How to Get One

IF YOU FOLLOW MY advice and decide to write a book on your freelance specialty, you will sooner or later require the services of a good agent. You will need an agent to sell your book to a publisher, or, if you manage to do this yourself, to negotiate a contract for you.

But getting an agent is not always easy. Many freelancers who are branching out into the world of book writing often consider this difficulty the chief obstacle to their success—after writing a good, marketable book in the first place.

There are two things about agents that every serious writer has got to understand:

1. What a good agent is and does, and
2. How, given those facts, you get one to represent you.

What an Agent Is

An agent, contrary to the beliefs—or at least the wishes—of many writers, cannot afford to work *pro bono* for writers whose books (even some very good books) have little chance of commercial success. A literary agent is a person who makes a living by placing a book with a publisher who will shell out the company's good money to publish it because it is thought to have a good likelihood of commercial success.

An agent may or may not love books, love the literary world, or even love writers. But man does not live by love alone; he must also

94

put food on the table. The agent, like you, has a mortgage payment, a car payment, kids to send to school, doctor bills, braces—in fact all the expenses that the rest of us have. Except the agent lives in New York or maybe Los Angeles, so his mortgage payment and all the other payments on the list are even higher than ours.

If he does not bring home the bacon—and fairly large slabs of it at that—he is soon in big financial trouble. It is not a business for the weak of heart. So he has little time to waste in unproductive effort. (If you live in New York or L.A. yourself, you might consider moving to the country to continue your writing career.)

An agent is also someone who lives by his wits. He is not salaried, has no company retirement fund, no sick leave, no paid-for hospitalization. He relies on two things, and two things only, to pay his bills:

1. His ability to pick from the many thousands of books submitted to his agency each year those few that he thinks he can sell and make a profit on, and
2. His intimate knowledge of the publishing business, of who is looking for what, of the current needs of as many publishing houses as he can gather information about.

The agent must choose books that not only get published but sell in large numbers after they are published. An agent lives by commissions alone, getting (usually) 15 percent of the royalties that the author earns. If the author earns little or nothing, the agent also earns little or nothing.

An Agent Is Born

How do you get to be an agent? You do it slowly, step by step, learning the business as you go. A typical career path is this: You start out as an editorial assistant at one of the larger publishing houses, probably in New York (although there are some sizeable publishers nowadays in other cities, such as F&W Publications—Writer's Digest Books—in Cincinnati, Ohio). You can also get a foot in the door by working as a first reader in one of the larger literary agencies. After a few years of working at this level and moving up the editorial ladder, the future agent is actively recommending and even acquiring manuscripts that his publisher will publish or his agency will represent. By now he has gotten a good feel for how the publishing business actually works (as distinct from the way it ought to work), has a long list of valuable contacts in a wide variety of publishing houses, and is tiring of the very low wages usually paid to editorial staff people.

And then one day he happens upon a manuscript that has everything going for it. Just the day before, he met with a publisher looking for that precise kind of thing. He says to the author, "Look. Let me handle this book for you. I think I know just who might be looking for something like this." The newly declared agent is successful in placing the book, negotiates a reasonable advance, and navigates the fine print of the publisher's contract and royalty schedule. The new agent is off and running. It is ever so much more gratifying than wading through the slush pile at Gotham Book Company on starvation wages. He never wants to see slush again (which may be the reason why, coming along some years later, you can't get him to read your over-the-transom manuscript).

The next step is career building, which consists mainly of getting high-dollar contracts for big name (or at least recognizable) authors. It also consists of building a reputation among the publishing companies as an agent who can always be trusted to bring solid manuscripts to fill their specific needs, and among writers as an agent who can get books published and get top dollar for them.

What the Agent Is Selling

If you are successful in finding an agent to represent you, he will get up to 20 percent of everything you make on your book. What

Of Agents and Pseudo-Agents

There are far more writers seeking agents than legitimate agents to supply the need. This mismatch between supply and demand can, and often does, offer a hard-to-resist opportunity for unscrupulous pseudo-agents who are constantly trying to cash in on the desire of writers for representation.

Warning signs: the pseudo-agent lives in a cornfield in Kansas and is not likely to attend networking lunches and events in metropolitan publishing centers. The pseudo-agent tells you that you are a fine writer but your manuscript needs work. He then offers to do this work for you at a hefty fee. Such a person may be a competent editor, but he is certainly not an agent. The pseudo-agent is actively selling his agenting services to writers: "new writers accepted," "let me help you publish your book," etc.

The Science Fiction and Fantasy Writers of America (SFWA) organization provides its members with a specific warning about these sharks who ply the waters of the literary world (www.sfwa.org).

The SFWA association caveats are very pointed and come from complaints and reports filed by their members. The association warns its members against agents who do the following things:

1. Charge upfront fees for services.
2. Promote agency editing services. Many of these are merely fronts for editing services.
3. Offer a "critique" for a sizeable fee.
4. Sell "adjunct" services, such as author websites, PR and promotion, and space in their catalogs.

Caveat emptor!

does he deliver in return? He delivers four very valuable things:

1. *Access.* Through his constant networking and his many personal contacts, he gives you access to the inner, decision making circles of the publishers with whom he deals. For fiction writers, the intermediary agent is a virtual necessity these days. Nonfiction writers have a somewhat easier time of it, but not by much.
2. *Day-to-day knowledge of publishing opportunities.* An agent provides day-to-day, constantly updated knowledge of what various publishing companies are looking for and even what individual editors at those houses are looking for.
3. *Knowledge of the internal dynamics of each publishing house.* Who's got the power? Who has the final say? A good agent will know this and package your book so that it has a better chance of successfully navigating the acquisitions process.
4. *Knowledge of publishing contracts and conditions.* A good agent's expertise is in contract negotiation. There is a lot to know, and you learn it by experience. Some innocuous-sounding clauses can have very serious, negative consequences for writers. After all, it is the publisher's contract. The publisher's attorneys drew it up, and it seeks to protect the publisher. First of all, how much will you get as an advance? An agent worth his salt will know what top dollar is and how to get it for you. Second, publishing contracts are laden with pitfalls that the unwary writer, acting on his own, probably would not see. Does your contract obligate you to submit your next book to the same publisher, whether or not you are satisfied with their efforts on your behalf? Does it specify that the royalties from other books of yours that they may publish go to defray any unearned advance on your earlier books before you get a dime? Do you give up reprint rights and electronic rights? If your book goes out of print, precisely when and how do all rights revert to you? If your book is marketed by the publisher through a print-on-demand tech-

nology, can it ever really go out of print? These are just some of the questions that an agent will sort out for his clients.

You may have a favorite, hometown lawyer to whom you can submit your contract for review, if it will make you feel more comfortable. Your country lawyer from Macon, Georgia will not know beans about publishing contracts, nor will the fancier one in Atlanta. The second will charge you more than the first one, but both will be pretty much useless to you. Your agent is the one you will rely on to negotiate your contract. His expertise in this area will more than pay for the percentage you pay out to him for his services.

What Agents Are Looking For (Do You Fill the Bill?)

How do you get an agent to work for you? There are two steps in the process. The first is to pull together a profile of the kinds of books that the agent is looking for, based on what you know about the agent. The second is to package yourself and your book to fit that profile.

Agents are looking for good books, right? Right enough, so long as you understand that for an agent a good book is, above all, a saleable book, a book that large numbers of people will buy. That's why the author of a great book of serious verse will never land an agent while the next Dr. Seuss will have them lined up at his door. The difference is that very few readers buy books of pure poetry but great numbers of them buy *The Cat in the Hat*. Agents are paid on commission. They get a 15- or 20-percent cut of your royalties. No sales, no royalties, no commissions. Poor sales, slim royalties. Great sales, everybody eats steak.

Agents are also looking for the promise of *continued productivity*. Agents want to represent writers who have the energy and will to write every day. In short, they are looking for professional writers. That's because they want to continue to represent you after they have placed the first book. If they are going to invest their time in you they want you, in turn, to invest your time and energy in producing new books that they can continue to sell to your publisher. Your productivity is an asset that is valuable to an agent. If you are a good writer you may attract an agent's attention. If you are a good and prolific writer, you have a far better chance of doing so. A ninety-nine-year-old man who has written a reasonably good first novel may get noticed. But most agents would not be interested. There is little prospect of an even better second and third novel down the line.

Agents want books with a "national" angle. Big-time agents want to sell to big-time publishers. And big-time publishers shy away from any book that smacks of a limited, regional market. It doesn't take much to get the "regional" label attached to your book; sometimes the title alone can do it.

Agents want books with a handle they can pitch to publishers: a niche, a newsworthy tie-in, subject matter that rides a crest of some pop-culture trend, a well-known name or place, or an endorsement or foreword from a well-known author ("The best book I ever read."—Stephen King).

Agents are looking for books with a dynamite title and a strong, reader-enticing first paragraph and chapter. They like writers who understand that the function of the first paragraph is to entice the reader to read the second paragraph, and so on through the book.

Agents are looking for books that lie within their field of specialization. Although this one is not an absolute, some agents do specialize in certain areas: romance, science fiction, how-to, New Age, etc. If you can position your book within an agent's specialty you may have a better chance of scoring a hit. You can find agents' specialties listed in *Literary Market Place*, in your library's reference room (make sure to consult a recent edition).

Three Questions Agents May Ask You

If you get a nibble from an agent and enter into negotiations with him, he will probably have some questions for you. These questions enable him to get a feel for your commitment to your writing career, your overall knowledge of your field (in the case of a nonfiction book) and your knowledge of what other authors have written and are selling in the same genre:

1. He might ask what you see as your target readership. Who do you think will read your book?
2. Market position. How is your book different from others in the same field or genre? How is it similar? In what ways is it unique?
3. What do you see as follow-up books that you intend to write, and when will you complete them?

The Reading Fee

It is widely believed that writers ought to avoid agents who charge a reading fee. It is true that you ought to look closely at anyone who does so, but some very reputable agents today are saying that a modest reading fee of some kind is necessary if they are going to look at all the submissions that come in to them. One of these is Richard Curtis, author of *The Business of Publishing* and widely respected in the field. Curtis points out that for an agent time is money, and neither he nor his fellow agents can afford the time that would be required to seriously consider all the thousands of writers' proposals that the mailman dumps out on their desks. A reading fee of $50 to $100 would enable them to do so. If that is the only fee, and if the agent is a member of the Association of Authors' Representatives, I see no reason not to pay it. But the minute anyone wants to charge more, or suggests a much heftier fee for "editing" or "manuscript preparation," pack your bag and run for cover.

Getting the Ball Rolling: How to Make Contact with an Agent

There are three ways to make preliminary contact with an agent. You must use all of them.

1. You meet an agent at a writer's conference, let them know that you have a series of books coming up that have market potential (although you let the agent decide that potential for himself) and that you've got the first book ready to send out. You ask: Could I send it to you? If the agent answers in the affirmative, you send the book along within the next few days. Your cover letter will begin something like, "We met recently at the Mystery Writer's Conference, and you were kind enough to ask me to send you my manuscript, (title)."

2. You have a friend who is a successful writer in the same field as you, and you ask that friend if he thinks his agent might be interested in seeing your manuscript. If he answers yes, you can ask him to make a preliminary contact for you. If he agrees, great. If he doesn't, you send your query along, and your cover letter begins, "My friend Stephen King suggested that you might be interested in the book I am writing . . . ."

3. You don't have either of these two opportunities, so you research the possibilities for yourself and send out query letters. Here's how to do it:

   • You can survey bookstores for books on topics similar to yours or in the genre in which you write. Note the author and publisher. Call either or both to find the name of the agent who made the sale. If you are good on the telephone you can usually find this out.

   • You can check through the listings in *Literary Market Place* for the names of agents who work in your field and send queries to five or ten of them at a time until you have either exhausted the list or found someone who will read your manuscript.

   • However you got the agent's name, the next step is to make contact and do it in a way most calculated to get the results you want. Agents cannot possibly pay attention to all the hopeful writers who contact them, so you've got to stand out, as best you can, from the crowd. A few paragraphs earlier we listed the things that agents are looking for. Now you present yourself to them as possessing each of these qualities. When you do this the agent will know that you are a writer who understands the business of writing. This alone will place you in a group apart, since 99 percent of writers who want to get published don't know how the publishing business really works.

Querying an Agent

You write a query letter to an agent in the same way you would to a publisher. In this letter you seek to demonstrate to the agent that you are a professional practitioner of the writing trade

- who writes well and frequently, and who has a lot more books coming down the pike;
- who understands market position, who has slanted his book to the broadest possible readership, and who has come up with a dynamite title;
- who has the knowledge and experience to write this particular book; and
- who has the literary talent to write this particular book.

Along with the letter, you send a brief sample of the text itself.

A Sample Letter

A few years ago, I had completed a book called *How to Make $100,000 a Year in Desktop Publishing* and was looking for an agent to help me land a publisher. I wrote the following letter to ten agents chosen from the *Literary Market Place* list. The letter was successful. I attracted and agent on the first go-round and placed the book with Betterway Publications, a subsidiary of F&W (Writer's Digest Books) Publications. The book became a Writer's Digest Book Club selection. Here is the letter:

Dear John Doe,

I went into business four years ago with a Mac Plus, a laser printer, and two used desks. (I've since added a second Mac.) Last year I grossed $800,000 in sales. This year I will top $1,000,000. Best of all, I did it with little or no cash up front.

In How to Make $100,000 a Year in Desktop Publishing *I tell other desktop publishers how they can do this, too. My book furnishes the desktop entrepreneur with all the information he or she needs to get started.*

I tell desktop computer owners how to make money publishing city and regional magazines; quality of life magazines; newcomers' guides; tourism guides; niche market tabloids; weekly newspapers; books (easier than you think, with no costs for inventory, using the desktop approach); and a city/county history. I tell them how to make money selling information by mail and on the Internet; how to deal with printers; how to design and sell advertising; how to hire the people they need at a price they can afford to pay; and how to market their services. No other book currently on the market does all these things.

I know these projects work because I have done them all myself. I have edited and published a weekly newspaper, a free-circulation shopper, a regional magazine, a quality-of-life magazine, a tourism guide, a newcomer guide, and an association directory. I sell information by mail. I have written and published five books and edited two others. My work has appeared in national and regional magazines, from Esquire *on down.*

I enclose a detailed outline. May I send you three completed chapters, with a view toward your representing me in the sale of this book? This book is the first of a series. I expect to complete the others at a rate of at least one each year.

Sincerely,
Tom Williams

Note that I state the premise of my book; I communicate something of its dynamism and style ("I went into business . . ." The lead paragraph of the query became the lead paragraph of the finished book). I summarized its contents and its slant (earn big bucks with no cash up front), I listed my credentials (have done them all myself), and I hinted at other books to come. The complete table of contents filled out the package.

You've got to do the same thing. If my book had been a novel, my style and approach would have been different, but I would have tried to say precisely the same kinds of things.

Use this letter as a template for creating your own agent-seeking queries. Type them up and send them out in batches of five or ten. Include a SASE, just as you would with a query sent directly to a publisher. If you have clips from good magazines, attach one or two of them to your letter, along with the title pages of any books you may have published.

Get an Agent by Publishing Your Own Book

There are more good writers than there are presses to publish them. The number of small and independent publishers—though greater than you may imagine—is still very small when compared to the number of books submitted to them. Mark Twain tells the story of an individual who, having gone to heaven, witnessed a celestial parade of the greatest poets in history. At the head of the file, just in front of Homer and Dante, marched a little shoemaker from the backwoods of Tennessee. He was the greatest of them all, Twain explained. He was unknown because he never managed to get published.

You need not let that happen to you. Today there is a sure way, once and for all, to end your own frustration at writing good work that you can't get into print: publish and sell it yourself. This is easier to do than you may think, and—contrary to what some may think—has become honorable. Publishing your own book is not a mysterious process; it is just a new skill with a gentle learning curve. And when you have done it once, you can do it again and again.

If the selling and marketing part worries you, keep in mind that you would bear the main burden of selling your books, no matter who published them.

In case there's any lingering doubt in your mind concerning the legitimacy of self-publication, let me take a moment here to set the record straight. Writers and others who have not been following the truly revolutionary changes in the publishing industry in the last few years may not be aware of the way in which the landscape has changed.

Far from being a back-door entry into the world of published authors, self-publication today is booming and is very respectable. As money becomes tighter and as major publishers focus more and more exclusively on the quest for blockbuster bestsellers, it has become inescapably clear that for books with limited sales potential— regional books, niche market books, specialty books—self-publication is not only an acceptable alternative but often the only alternative. If you believe in your book and want to see it in print, bring it out yourself, utilizing the methods and strategies of self-publication.

Not Just an Agent, but a Good Agent

Not all agents are born equal, and there is many a scam out there. You can be pretty sure that your agent is professionally reputable and effective if he is a member of the Association of Authors' Representatives (AAR), as you will see from the following list of membership requirements (summarized from www.aar-online.org):

1. Membership in the AAR is restricted to those agents who have devoted full time to the practice of their profession for at least two years prior to joining the organization.
2. Membership in the AAR is restricted to agents who were "principally responsible for executed agreements concerning the grant of publication, translation or performance rights" for at least ten literary properties during the eighteen months

prior to joining the organization.

3. Membership is restricted to those agents who agree in writing to conduct their activities according the AAR canon of ethics. The canon of ethics can be read in full at the AAR website, www. aar-online.org.

These are quite stringent requirements that will eliminate beginners, scammers, and those whose agenting is merely a sideline.

Questions You Want to Ask

Every day someone else is setting up as an agent. Why not? The money looks good and you really don't have to work hard for it. Or so they think. These amateur—when not outright con-artist—agents have few if any contacts, have never made a major deal, and often live in unlikely places like the unexplored territories of Montana or the backwoods of Georgia. Not many publishing industry luncheons or networking cocktail parties going on out there.

But the difficulty of finding someone to represent you and your work can be so disheartening that writers are easily tempted to sign up with anyone who professes an interest in them. They are too easily led to believe that anyone advertising himself as an agent will actually be able to place their book with a publisher. But this is not likely in a great many cases. An agent who has not put together substantial deals is a wannabe agent, just as a writer who writes seldom and poorly is a wannabe writer.

So how do you know who's good at finding publishing deals and who's not? There is a way. Once an agent expresses an interest in you, there are some questions you should ask. The following list was developed by the AAR and will go a long way toward separating the literary wheat from the chaff:

1. Are you a member of the Association of Authors' Representatives?

2. How long have you been in business as an agent?

3. Do you have specialists at your agency who handle movie and television rights? Foreign rights?

4. Do you have subagents or corresponding agents in Hollywood and overseas?

5. Who in your agency will actually be handling my work? Will the other staff members be familiar with my work and the status of my business at your agency? Will you oversee or at least keep me apprised of the work that your agency is doing on my behalf?

6. Do you issue an agent-author agreement? May I review the language of the agency clause that appears in contracts you negotiate for your clients?

7. How do you keep your clients informed of your activities on their behalf?

8. Do you consult with your clients on any and all offers?

9. What are your commission rates? What are your procedures and time frames for processing and disbursing client funds? Do you keep different bank accounts separating author funds from agency revenue? What are your policies about charging clients for expenses incurred by your agency?

10. When you issue 1099 tax forms at the end of each year, do you also furnish clients upon request with a detailed account of their financial activity, such as gross income, commissions and other deductions, and net income, for the past year?

11. In the event of your death or disability, what provisions exist for my continued representation?

12. If we should part company, what is your policy about handling any unsold subsidiary rights in my work?

Legitimate Agent Charges

Although the AAR asks its members not to charge reading fees, some expenses incurred by the agency may be charged back to the writer. These are such charges as the cost of copying your manuscript as it becomes shopworn, mailing costs, and some other routine out-of-pocket expenses. Clarify with your agent what these charge-back items will be.

In Sum:

The One, Two, Three of Getting an Agent

1. Understand that an agent makes his living representing authors who write books that publishers will publish and that readers will buy.
2. Understand that if you want an agent to represent you, you must convince him that you are an author who writes books that publishers will publish and that readers will buy and in large numbers.
3. Let your agent know that you are not a one-book wonder; that there will be a steady stream of as-good-or-better books coming down the pike.

— 9 —

Will They Steal My Idea?
and Other Scary Questions

Your book is both interesting and original. Unfortunately, the part that is original is not interesting, and the part that is interesting is not original.

—Samuel Johnson

WHEN I GET TO the part of my freelance writing seminars where I explain how to write a query or book proposal, at least one writer in the room will raise a hand to ask this heartfelt question: "How do I know they won't steal my idea?"

Perhaps you have asked this question yourself. And why not? After all, it is your idea. You thought it, wrote it, polished it, and now you are ready to try to get it published. The last thing you want is to get a rejection slip, followed by a similar article over someone else's byline a few months later.

Some writers seen almost paralyzed by the fear of losing the products of their minds and hearts to faceless, unscrupulous idea-pirates plying the waters of the literary world. For them, entrusting an article idea to some unknown editor many miles away is a little like sending a beloved child out to deliver a bouquet of roses to a suspected mass murderer. For this kind of writer, querying is a very painful catch-22: they can't get published without sending their ideas out for consideration, but if they send ideas out they risk (they fear) losing them to people who do not have ideas of their own. So what's the truth of the matter? Are article ideas really stolen? Seldom? Often?

My Own Experience

I am happy to report that in my thirty-five years as a magazine editor and freelance writer, I have had no ideas stolen, stolen no ideas, and I have not known anyone else who has done so. If the idea-pirates are really out there, they have never sailed my way.

Moreover, pirates or no, what choice do you have? You've got to spread your ideas around, too. Otherwise you're like a farmer who refuses to sow his seed for fear the birds will eat them. He succeeds in protecting his seed from the vagaries of the natural world, but he also prevents them from germinating and bearing fruit. If you want to be a writer, you've got to send your ideas out, or they just rot in your mind like the fearful farmer's unsown seed will eventually do in his barn.

Ideas and Words

But here's the good news: ideas are usually not all that important in themselves. It's what your particular and personal skill as a writer brings to them that counts. Pick up a few of your favorite magazines and leaf through. How many article ideas strike you as truly original. A few? Less than that? None? I'd vote for none. These articles were bought because they were timely and well-written, and precisely slanted to the market, not because they were unique.

Here's a story that illustrates the relationship of ideas and words. The French poet Stéphane Mallarmé was asked by a younger writer where he got the ideas for his poems. "You don't make poems with ideas," Mallarmé replied. "You make them with words."

So it doesn't really matter if someone does copy your idea; without resorting to outright plagiarism, they still can't steal your style. It is the rhythm, the images, the sounds of the words—even the way they look on the page—that makes a poem or a first-rate article or story. The idea is secondary, except that it needs to be one of interest to most readers.

The same thing is true of all writing. Don't believe me? Try this idea: "Don't give all your worldly goods to your children. They may not love you as much as you love them." Expressed this way, the idea is bland, flat. But this same idea, when dressed out in Shakespeare's words, becomes *King Lear*. How many books have been based on this idea: "A young man and a young woman fall in love, but the natural course of their passion is blocked and tragedy ensues." How many hundreds—thousands—of books have been based on this idea, ranging from *Romeo and Juliet* to *An American Tragedy* to five million Harlequin romances? The idea is the same, but the books themselves could scarcely be more different.

The idea of the "gratuitous act" has fascinated modern writers. In this scenario a person commits an act of violent murder, not for any rational motive, but simply because it can be done. That is a very clear and simple idea, but in the hands of different writers it finds very different and complex expression: Dostoevsky in *Crime and Punishment*, André Gide in *The Caves of the Vatican*, and Truman Copote in his "nonfiction novel" *In Cold Blood*. It is difficult to imagine three more different books, but the same basic idea informs them all.

Ideas and Editors

In the publishing business, editors see the same ideas over and over again. This is because there just not that many of them. At the most basic level are love, hate, greed, ambition, and the need for security. Then there are the subcategories: pure love, erotic love, selfless love, lust; hatred of oneself, hatred of another, hatred of a race; greed for money, for land, for power; ambition to achieve political power, worldly status, heroic stature; financial security, physical security, emotional security.

That's barely a dozen ideas, and they cover almost everything in human experience. So it is not surprising that editors see them again and again.

Slant and Style

No, your idea is not likely to tempt an editor to steal it. Most editors got where they are because their own minds are fairly brimming over with ideas of their own. Neither is a shortage of ideas a problem for most experienced writers. The problem is not a shortage of ideas, but a shortage of the time required to develop them all.

Editors are looking for two things: a new slant on the same basic truths of human experience that have always interested readers; and a strong, original style capable of dressing out those ideas in words that will give freshness and originality to their expression. No one has the time or the need to steal ideas. Good writers are the rare commodity, and if you approach an editor with a fresh slant on a subject he likes in a query letter that shows him you can write well enough to bring your idea to life, you couldn't drive him off with a baseball bat. It is you, not your idea, that mainly interests him, because you package that rare combination of imagination and talent that he is looking for.

When It Looks Like Theft, but Isn't

So where do the stories of stolen ideas come from? Many have the air of urban legend about them, the "Someone I know told me," or "It happened to this friend of a friend of mine"—the kind of thing that can give pause, but is ultimately unverifiable, probably because it never happened.

Other stories may indeed have happened but are not really instances of idea theft. Here are four reasons why that is true:

1. *Simultaneous Invention.* In this case, two individuals, not in contact with one another, give birth to the same idea or clusters of ideas at roughly the same time. This is not a new phenomenon. It happens all the time, and at every level of endeavor. Isaac Newton in England and Gottfried Leibnitz in Germany developed infinitesimal calculus during the same

years, independent of one another. What wonder, then, that two writers, unknown to one another, should write an article about a new scheme for making millions from a home-based office. Both articles are submitted to the same magazine. One is accepted and the other declined. Did the same editor see both versions? Not likely. Was one better written than the other? Undoubtedly. Was one slanted more precisely to the readership of the magazine in question? Very likely.

In any case it is simultaneous invention and not idea theft that is going on. An idea is simply in the air, and several freelancers, independently of one another, jump on it and try to market it. It is entirely possible that this is the source of many "stolen idea" complaints. An editor has several versions of the same thing on his desk. He chooses one and rejects the other. Several months later the rejected writer sees an article on a theme similar to that of his own piece in the magazine. He raises a hue and cry, claiming that his idea has been stolen. But he is wrong and suffering from a bad case of simultaneous invention.

2. *New Editor.* Revolving editorial chairs are a hazard of the writing business. What one editor rejects, his or her successor may like very much. Further, there will surely be little contact between the two of them. This means that Editor 2 is completely unaware of the fact that Editor 1 has just rejected your version of an article idea that another freelancer has just submitted.

3. *Bad Timing.* You submit your idea for a summer vacation article at a time when the staff is busy lining up their Christmas issue. Your article is overlooked. When attention turns to vacation articles, yours is gone and that of another writer is on hand. Though both articles deal with the same topic, the writer whose article is currently on the desk gets the assignment.

4. *Bad Query.* Your article idea was a good one, but your query failed to convince the editors (poor organization, misspelled

words, general lack of attention to detail) that you could do the job. It may also be that your query was a good one but your style and slant were inconsistent with the tone of the magazine. Your article is rejected for this reason. Another article query, having met those standards, is accepted.

These are just a few of the ways in which an article similar to yours can appear after you have submitted a query without anyone's being at fault.

What about Copyright?

In the publishing business, the standard bar against the theft of intellectual property is the international copyright convention. Following this convention, the vast majority—but not all—of literate and literary countries worldwide join in recognizing the sole right of an author to enjoy the ownership and benefits of his or her literary works, unless he has voluntarily signed that right over to others.

For most of the twentieth century, copyright law in the United States was defined by the Copyright Act of 1909, which granted protection to the author of a work for a period of twenty-eight years, this initial period of protection being renewable for another twenty-eight years. In the event that the copyright was not renewed, all protection expired, and the work in question passed into the pubic domain. Until the late nineteenth century no one's books, let alone ideas, were secure. Unauthorized editions of popular works could be and were published around the world, with no benefits at all going to the author.

Writers enjoy much more protection from present-day copyright laws than they ever enjoyed before. The new version of our copyright law went into effect in 1978. Under the new law, copyright protection exists for the author's lifetime plus fifty years, bringing the United States into line with the copyright laws of England and some other countries. Furthermore, copyright protection is said to exist from the moment that a work, in whole or in part, exists in concrete form: handwritten, typed, or output from a computer. Technically, copyright registration is no longer necessary, but in the absence of a certificate of copyright issued by the Copyright Office of the Library of Congress, one's rights under the law are much more difficult to assert—perhaps even impossible.

To err on the side of caution you may wish to have your articles copyrighted before you submit them. To save money (the copyright registration fee is currently $30) you can submit more than one article at a time and cover them with one certificate. You do not have to wait until you have the certificate in hand before you send your piece out. Simply type *"Copyright © 200X by (Your Name)"* after the last line of text, then send off your copyright application.

A certificate of copyright is easy to obtain. One has only to send two copies of the literary product, a copyright application, and a check for (as of this writing) $30 to the Office of Copyrights at the Library of Congress. You can get details and download application forms online at www.loc.gov/copyright/.

When you are published in a magazine or newspaper, you may believe that a copyright has been registered in your name by the publishing magazine, but this is not true. There is a notice of copyright on the masthead of the publication, but this covers only in-house materials and the organization, design, and sequence of the articles it contains. Because of this fact, you will often see a copyright notice when reading syndicated columns in your newspaper.

What Copyright Does Not Cover

Although a certificate of copyright is the most basic and effective protection available for a literary work, it does not cover some things:

- It does not, for instance, cover the title of your work.

- It does not prevent persons from quoting a paragraph or two (the exact amount is ill-defined) under the fair use doctrine. Thus a college student preparing a term paper on *Hamlet* can, without fear of copyright violation, quote a hundred or so words from another critic's study of that same play. Anyone who wants to quote more extensively than that will have to write to the holder of the copyright and ask permission to do so and pay whatever fee, if any, may be asked.
- It does not protect a basic plot idea; it only protects your work expressing that plot through your words.

Trademarks and Fair Trade Practices

Copyright law does not protect a title, but there may be other laws that do so in certain, well-defined cases. These usually have to do with violations of laws governing fair trade practices. Another person may not legally appropriate your title (though you would have to go to court to prevent it) if your title is part and parcel of a larger marketing presence.

Such titles are said to be the equivalent of brand names. A well-known example today is the *For Dummies* and *Idiot's Guide* series that are seen in all the bookstores. *Cliff's Notes* is another. I have written a series of reference guides for writers called *Little Blue Sourcebooks™ for Writers and Self-Publishers*. Note that I include the small "™" after "*Sourcebooks*" to warn others that this is a "branded" or trademarked series.

A Work Made for Hire

There is another part of the copyright law that freelancers must be very careful of: the "work made for hire." In the past there have been many controversies about ownership of texts written for others, for which the writer got paid. Often the person who commissioned the writing considered that he owned the work outright, while the writer also felt some ownership rights.

The Copyright Law of 1978 draws a very clear distinction between work to which a writer gives up all rights in return for a fee, and other work to which a writer retains rights. The Copyright Act refers to the former (no-rights project) as a "work made for hire." If you see this phrase in any agreement you are asked to sign, you must understand that you are selling your work outright and will retain no further relationship to it. In many cases, this is a perfectly acceptable arrangement. In others it may not be.

There may be cases in which you want to utilize the "for hire" distinction for your own purposes. A friend of mine used to hire students to work as editorial interns. They did research and produced some boilerplate for a series of guidebooks she was publishing. To make certain that none of her interns raised a fuss when they saw a paragraph or two of their own in a longer piece under my friend's byline, she had them all sign a work-for-hire agreement before they went to work.

Work-for-hire arrangements must be explicitly stated in a written agreement to be valid.

New Dangers: The Electronic Frontier

As long as the writing business consisted wholly of print publications, any problems of ownership were pretty much dealt with by the Copyright Law of 1978. But now, with the vast, untamed, and still mostly unexplored territories of electronic publishing before us, it is an unwise writer who does not learn what the real dangers of this new frontier are and how to protect himself against them. Most of these are the products of the new electronic techniques for propagating print media: websites, e-books, and their kindred substitutes for ink on paper.

In the electronic jungle you are dealing with rights pirates rather than idea pirates. And the rights pirates really do exist. Rights pirates make their living not by stealing your idea but by poaching on your right to profit from that idea in its written form. For instance, you are paid for the initial publication or "first serial rights" but receive nothing from later uses of your work when the publication that bought it, unjustly claiming the right to do so, republishes you article electronically or by some other means. The National Writer's Union (www.nwu.org) and the American Association of Journalists and Authors (www.asja.org), the two leading advocates for freelance writers, are currently working to bring fair compensation to the writer in these cases. Check their websites for latest details of ongoing litigation.

A Minor Case of E-Grabbing

Here is a minor case of electronic rights grabbing from my own experience. It was not important to me, since I wrote the piece primarily for public relations purposes and to gain visibility for my publishing business in the community to which I had just moved.

I recently set up my office in Savannah, Georgia, having relocated from Fort Lauderdale. My business—Williams & Company—designs, publishes, and sometimes even ghostwrites family and local history. I contacted the editor of a tabloid supplement to the *Savannah Morning News* called *Coastal Senior* and proposed an article, "How to Write (and Publish) a Living Family History." The editor liked the idea and told me how much he would pay. I accepted the deal. I wrote the piece and it was duly published.

A week later the editor who had bought my piece sent me a contract to sign so that he could send me a check. This *ex post facto* contract, I discovered, granted the newspaper not only first serial rights, but all other rights, including electronic rights, web rights, and the right to use and distribute my piece by any other means now in existence or which might one day come into existence. Talk about a broad grant of rights!

The same thing will happen to you, if you don't take care to read the small print. Most of us achieve some kind of freelance profitability by recycling articles, by selling them more than once to non-competing markets, or by recycling them later in books. A contract like the one that newspaper sent me makes such multiple uses technically illegal. Under the terms of this agreement, if I used my article again I would be in violation of copyright and the newspaper would not.

Fortunately this piece, for me, was a throwaway. I wrote it to achieve some publicity and name recognition and did not intend to market it elsewhere. Nevertheless and as a matter of principle, I doubt that I would have signed the agreement giving up all rights had I seen it before publication.

Life after Life

You have written an article, and it has been published. You enjoy your moment of success, add a title to your bibliography, tear sheets to your file, and a check to your bank account. End of story.

Not necessarily. Your article may very well have a much longer life that you ever suspected. These days, a so-called "electronic database" may pick it up and store it, along with thousands of other articles, in its files. When a client calls the database company and requests information on a given topic, the database's computers spew out all relevant info—including a copy of your article. The database is paid by its client, but you do not receive a cent in compensation. The publication in which your article first appeared may have "sold" the right to use your article to the database in the first place. Again, you received no payment. Or the publication itself may run a website on which it archives your article for perusal over a virtually unlimited period of time.

The National Writers Union reports that there are "more than 100 NWU members . . . protesting the sale of their work at high prices to users without a dime being paid to writers."

Plagiarism

A final way that a dishonest writer can perform some intellectual picking of your intellectual pockets is by plagiarizing your work. The plagiarist doesn't just steal your ideas. He steals your words as well. Plagiarism is not widespread in professional writing and commercial publishing because it is so easy to spot, so easy to prove, and so expensive to remedy.

The good news is that in all but a few rare cases plagiarism is little more than a nuisance. It is common among high school and college students faced with a term paper deadline on a topic that they know absolutely nothing about. For some, the rich resources of the Internet have made this kind of "borrowing" too tempting to resist. It is now beginning to be controlled by special computer programs available to teachers that are designed to detect electronically plagiarized texts. (See www.plagiarism.com.) This classroom copying, though reprehensible, is not likely to harm anyone financially.

Plagiarism is not always intentional. In the past year, two well-known historians, Doris Kearns Goodwin and Stephen Ambrose, were found to have used materials in their work lifted from other writers without attribution or note. Neither of these writers needed to lift text written by others, but most prolific scholars and authors of extensive, broadly sweeping narratives routinely employ research assistants to do legwork for them and gather relevant notes and references.

Some of these notes more than likely found their way into the finished text because the attribution had been omitted at the research assistant level. Few would claim that the writers whose work was stolen were actually harmed by the theft. Those most harmed by the revelations were Kerns and Ambrose themselves, who were wounded where it hurt most: in their reputations.

Sometimes, though, the plagiarism is more extensive and much less excusable. H. G. Wells, the turn-of-the-century British author of such mega-hits as *The Time Machine*, *The War of the Worlds*, and *The Invisible Man*, published a book called *The Outline of History*. I remember reading this book during my college years, back in the 1950s.

I wondered how it was possible for one man to have so many facts at his fingertips.

As it turned out, it was not possible after all, at least not in Wells's case. He plagiarized a good part of his book from a Canadian author, Florence Deeks, whose own outline of history he had read in manuscript form. This affair is the subject of a recent book by A.B. McKillop, *The Spinster and the Prophet: H.G. Wells, Florence Deeks, and the Case of the Plagiarized Text*. (New York, Four Walls Eight Windows, 2002).

The POD Blues

POD (print-on-demand) scams are not technically idea theft, but you may feel an unfriendly hand deep in your pocket just the same. More importantly, the blood, sweat, and tears that you put into molding your idea into a finished book may be more or less permanently shunted off into a literary dead end.

 Technically, print-on-demand is simply a means of production, a way to produce very limited numbers of books at an affordable price. This technology is available to anyone who chooses to use it and has been a boon to self-publishers and others who want to test the market before committing sizeable sums of money to the printing of large numbers of books.

Most printers who offer print-on-demand services have nothing to do with the actual business of publishing. However, this technology has been adopted by a number of companies that advertise themselves as "POD publishers." The most cursory search on the Internet will produce a list of many such companies.

Thus, "print-on-demand" has come to refer not only to a way of printing books but to a way of publishing them as well. As an example of POD as a publishing business, let's look at a fictitious company that I will call "Starbound Books." Though the company is fictitious, the facts presented are real and can be found, with minor variations, in the brochures and on the websites of all major POD publishers. It is not difficult to get published at Starbound. If you have written a book that does not transgress the laws of libel or decency, Starbound will undoubtedly publish it.

Here is the way it typically works. A writer, frustrated by his or her inability to find a publisher for a manuscript, sees an advertisement for a web-based publisher who offers to publish any book, in print or e-book formats, for what seems to be a small fee, usually a few hundred dollars. The publisher further offers to pay the writer a royalty of 20 to 40 percent on books sold and to sell books to the writer himself at a discount of as much as 50 percent off the retail price. The publisher also offers to pay the writer a hefty percentage of any money received through the sale of subsidiary rights. So what's wrong with this deal? Here are just a few ways this agreement can go wrong for the unwary writer:

- The publisher does no editing, and so the published books suffers greatly—often fatally—from the lack of professional editorial input.
- The publisher uses a template design format into which he forces many different kinds of books. The one chosen for your book may not be at all suitable. Reviewers who pick up an ill-designed book, usually put it down again just as quickly.
- The publisher does nothing at all to market the author's book. This fact is explicit in the presentations made by leading POD publishers.
- The author's book is not likely to be reviewed in any substantial and important review media. Why? Since the POD publishers will publish any book, no matter how badly written it may be, most review sources routinely set them aside as not worthy of their scarce editorial time.
- Many POD publishers will ask that the writer sign away far more of his rights than is called for. They do this so that, in the rare instance that one of their titles becomes a strong seller—in spite of the fact that they have done nothing to make

it do so—they, as publisher, will stand to reap a substantial part of any profits made.

- The POD publisher offers entry-level services at very attractive rates, often as little as a couple of hundred dollars. However, if you want any custom design features, proofreading, editing, or individual cover design this base price rises very rapidly.

So if the vast majority of Starbound's books are amateurish productions virtually guaranteed not to sell, how does the company make money? Simple. It sells printed books directly to its authors at discounts ranging from 19 percent to 50 percent off list price.

This is a very profitable arrangement. Let's say that the print version of a book retails for $19.95 and is sold to the author at a 40 percent discount, or $11.97. If this hypothetical book has 200 pages, printing costs, at the very most, are $3. Thus Starbound Books nets a profit of $8.97 on books sold to its own authors. Let's say, further, that Starbound Books has 1,000 authors each month, each of whom orders 25 copies of his or her book for friends, relatives, and local reviewers. One thousand multiplied by 25 equals 25,000. This figure multiplied by $8.97 equals $224,250, producing an annual income of $2,691,000. When you consider that Starbound Books, since it is a POD publisher, has no investment in inventory, no need for warehousing or fulfillment services, and that the whole enterprise, once set up, can do business almost entirely in the thin air of hyperspace, the net profit is substantial.

Starbound doesn't have to sell your books to anyone else to make money. They make it by selling them to you.

Why a Union?
I have suggested that readers go to the web site of the National Writers Union, find out what they are up to, and consider joining. I suggest this because there is power in numbers. Individually, writ-

ers have little chance of winning a legal battle with a large, power-ful, and above all well-financed business or corporation. In the American court system, the guy with the most money almost al-ways wins. That's why serious writers should band together and pool their resources to create legal precedents that will help protect them from the kind of literary piracy that the database companies are now practicing and from the depredations of unscrupulous writ-ers like H.G. Wells.

— 10 —

How to Sell Information on the Internet

JUST A FEW YEARS ago I would have called this chapter "How to Sell Information by Mail." Today, the focus has shifted to the digital world. Freelancers are discovering that they can make money by selling their work on the internet. They can do this through websites they design themselves and put up on the Internet at a cost of less than $20 a month, or even at no charge at all. My own site, currently hosted by Doteasy.com, is free. Sometimes such websites are wildly successful and bring in large sums of money each month. Sometimes they bring in a very welcome $500 to $1,000 a month. Sometimes they don't work too well and have to be tweaked to prime the sales pump.

The World Wide Web: A Chaos of Opportunities for Writers

Chaos? It certainly seems so to anyone working the web today. The opportunities the Internet offers expand daily, and it is impossible to know what tomorrow will bring. Still, I have jumped in and am paddling fiercely, and I advise you to do the same. There is little cost beyond learning how to use a web editor like Adobe GoLive, Dreamweaver, or FrontPage so that you can design and administer your own site.

I have one website that I have been selling information on for three years now: www.PubMart.com. On it I sell my books and my *Little Blue Sourcebooks*™, how-to guides for the freelance writer, covering many of the same topics you have read about in this book but also going beyond that into the area of self-publishing.

Ten years ago, I had never heard of the Internet and seven years ago I had never heard of the World Wide Web. In those days, I sold my information books and manuals by mail order—a much more expensive and much less effective way of doing business than selling through a website. I had to place ads or send out flyers, print my products, and hope for the best. This all cost real money. Today, I put it all on my website for less money a month than two or three Big Mac dinners at McDonald's. This doesn't mean that you are automatically going to make money without learning the ropes, but it does mean that learning curve is going to be pretty much cost-free. The profit potential is there, but the risk is gone.

The Web Is in a Constant State of Change

The web is constantly changing and has yet to define itself. After three years of working with it I realize that I know as little about what will happen tomorrow—or next month—as Cortes knew about the empire of the Aztecs when he got off his galleon at Vera Cruz and began his advance on Mexico City. This example may be a little strained, but I like it because, like Mexico City for Cortes, the Internet is absolutely new and uncharted territory. No one knows where it is going in the long run or even where it can go.

So how can I tell you how to make money selling information on the web? Well, I am currently doing it. And if the final structure or business model of the web remains unknown, the principles that enable you to sell your work on it are clear. You will need four things:

1. Information products, articles, and books that help people solve problems that are important to them, meet needs that are so far unmet, and reach goals that they may envision but do not yet know how to reach.
2. Information products that will appeal to a well-defined and targeted group of buyers who want, need, and can expect to

profit from the knowledge you are making available to them.

3. A website from which you can sell your information products.

4. Alternatively, a list of other people's Websites from which you can sell your information products.

Information Sells: A Story from Pre-Internet Days

Let me tell you how I came to understand the great profit potential of informational books, booklets, and manuals. Back in the pre-internet dark ages, some twenty-five years ago, I bought a weekly newspaper in the small college town of Davidson, North Carolina. I had edited a magazine and published books out of my office at the university where I was then teaching. At the university, publishing was a breeze. It was a breeze because I did not really have to make a living at it. My full professor's salary was generous. Anything beyond that was pure gravy.

The weekly newspaper business, I quickly discovered, was another matter altogether. In buying the *Gazette* I had burnt all my bridges, resigning my teaching position and the wonderfully regular salary it provided. I had to make it week by week on the cash that ad sales generated. The financial safety net was gone forever. I was immediately confronted with the task of meeting a weekly payroll, with my own name at the top of the list of those who needed a check. It was, I learned, a simple proposition: no profit, no pay.

I scoured every nook and cranny of my little journalistic kingdom for possible sources of cash. I took inventory of the possibilities. Along with the newspaper, I had acquired a darkroom, a decent graphic arts camera, and an ancient Multilith 1250 duplicator press. I decided that I would go to work doing job printing—turning out letterheads, envelopes, brochures, and advertising flyers when I wasn't busy meeting the deadlines of my weekly newspaper.

But how would I market my printing services? Davidson, after all, had fewer than 3,000 inhabitants. The nearby towns of Huntersville and Cornelius, also in my trade area, were even smaller. I was puzzling over this problem one day when the postman brought the morning's mail. On the top of the stack of the day's assortment of catalogs and brochures was a newsprint publication called *The Printer's Shopper*. It was a wishbook full of the odds and ends that printers require to do business: glues, racks, light tables, clamps, pica rules, T-squares, business forms, encyclopedias—thousands of prosaic but fascinating and useful items for the small print shop.

Idly thumbing through, I stopped cold when, at the top of page 63, I saw an advertisement for a book that promised to solve the problem of building an income in the printing business. Written by Owen C. Brantley, it was entitled *144 Ways to Sell Printing by Mail*. The book did not promise you some ways, mind you, nor a few ways, but a full 144 separate and distinct ways to get people to pay you money to do their printing for them no matter where they lived.

The offer was irresistible. I had a problem. Owen C .Brantley wanted to tell me how to solve it. It was precisely the information I needed. The price ($29.50) was relatively steep for those days, but if the book lived up to expectations, I felt certain that it would make money for me. As cash poor as I was, I wrote out a check and sent in my order.

The book was delivered two weeks later. It was not much to look at—just a sheaf of mimeographed pages held together in a cardboard binder. I did not care. It was the information I was interested in, not the design of the book. And the information was there. I was a satisfied customer. I had just bought information I needed by mail.

Nearly twelve years later, in an entirely different business in an entirely different town, I again received a copy of *The Printer's Shopper* in the morning mail. On page 41? You guessed it, an ad for *144 Ways to Sell Printing by Mail*, by Owen C. Brantley. For twelve years (that I know of) Brantley has been steadily selling his book to printers nationwide. All this time he has been bringing in a steady profit. (Nobody continues to advertise a product that people don't buy.)

The Light Dawns

It finally dawned on me that the real way to make money was not to stand over my little press printing Sunday programs and envelopes for the local church but to take a page out of Brantley's book and create and sell how-to manuals. In the years that followed I wrote and published *How to Make $100,000 a Year in Desktop Publishing*; *How to Publish City Magazines, Tourism Guides and Newcomer Guides*; *How to Start and Publish Weekly Newspapers, Niche-Market Tabloids and Free-Circulation Shoppers*; *Poet Power: The Practical Poet's Guide to Getting Published (and Self-Published)*; *How to Publish Real Estate and Apartment Guides*; *Publish Your Own Magazine, Guidebook, or Weekly Newspaper* and many similar publications.

What Kind of Information Can You Sell?

The information products you sell can be packaged in three formats:

1. *Books and manuals*: You can divide any piece of writing more than 20,000 words long (and sometimes shorter) into chapters and sell it as a book or how-to manual. Such books should always include a rich appendix of sources, a guide to other books on the subject, a glossary of special terminology that may be peculiar to the field, and an index and other content-enhancing materials. You will sell your books and manuals as e-books on the web, but you may also make them available to libraries and bookstores through inventory-free print-on-demand publishing with companies like Lightning Source, a subsidiary of Ingram Book Company (you can check this out at www.lightningsource.com).

2. *Special reports*: These are article-length pieces that tell readers

how to solve a single problem. They can be sold for $5 to $10, depending on content. You can turn out one or two of these a day if you need to. A special report for sale on my website is typical: *The Query Letter That Never Fails*. Special reports can be sold on the web as e-books. Since they are short, they are quickly and easily downloadable. Special reports can be very valuable to the reader and they are priced to sell as impulse purchases.

3. *Tips booklets*: These little booklets are often an easy sale. Paulette Ensign is a successful promotor, writer, and publisher of such booklets. It's worth browsing through her website (www.tipsbooklets.com) to check out her techniques and methods. You may be amazed at what is possible. I have a friend named Ron Gallo, a fishing guide, who writes a column for several community papers in South Florida. I helped him edit and prepare his first book, *How to Catch More Bass*, for publication in print and as an e-book. I also suggested that he do a few tips booklets. He just sold a hundred copies of his first one (*110 Tips on Teaching Your Kids to Fish*) to the Coral Springs, Florida, Department of Recreation. They cost him $.50 to produce. He sold them for $4.95, for a profit of $445 on the deal. He will sell dozens more every time he does one of his famous fishing clinics. Ron has nine more tips booklets and four books on the way. He sells them in print versions and as e-books on his website.

You will become quite proficient in recognizing good, saleable ideas for your book, reports and booklets, as you become more involved in business. But whatever your ideas, they should share these two essential ingredients:

1. The best ideas will pull orders from a small percentage of a large, well-targeted readership. Here's what you are dealing with. Only a certain percentage of those who read about your book will want it; of those who want it, only a certain per-

centage will have the money to buy it; of those who want it and can afford it, only a certain percentage will take the time and trouble to order it. By this time you have whittled your pool of potential buyers down considerably. The larger the number of prospects you start with, the greater the number of buyers you will attract. For instance, you may have some very hot information on, say, "How to Invest in Real Estate on the Island of Martinique." No matter how good the book, the number of people who can see themselves engaging in that activity is relatively small. The topic, "How to Make $100,000 a Year Selling Information on the Internet," will appeal to a greater number of people. Joe Karbo's famous mail order book, *Lazy Man's Way to Wealth,* appealed to even more. That's why Karbo is a millionaire today.

2. The best ideas appeal to a well-defined niche market and allow for the development and writing of many related products that will appeal to the same niche. My website, PubMart.Com, will appeal to all those who want to make money writing, a fairly large group of people. This book is the lead title on the site, and there are many other topics that I can write about that will be of interest to this same group of people. Visitors attracted to my site by the freelance theme may also be interested in my other manuals, such as *The Query Letter That Never Fails, Tom Williams's Book Writing System*, and *Perils and Pitfalls of POD Publishing.*

Trolling for Information

What information can you publish and where do you get it? Start with yourself. What do you know how to do that others would want to know about? Since I am a writer and a successful desktop publisher, I have written widely on that subject. There is a virtually inexhaustible supply of information that I can impart and be paid for.

There are other topics, too, in my personal inventory that I can muster for sale. Some years ago I did a lot of reading in the field of psychic research. Today, with very little effort, I could put together a manual on what has become known as channeling—the current name for the phenomenon of mediumship. A booklet called "How to Channel Information from Higher Worlds" might be profitable. To find out whether people will buy it, I can advertise it on my website before I ever put a word on paper. If the ad pulls an adequate response I can quickly write the piece and send it out to my customers.

Since I have started several small businesses, and worked with the Small Business Administration in doing so, I could also write a booklet on "How the U. S. Government Will Help Finance Your Business Idea."

These are all subjects I know about and have researched at one time or another. You may find that you have accumulated information that is saleable, too, if you take the time to dig for it. Your idea does not have to be unique to be profitable. This is a good thing, since there are very few new ideas in the world. However, any idea can be packaged in a new and attractive way. We all bring a different slant, a different perspective to our information, and this difference can be valuable. As writers, this individuality of presentation is our stock in trade.

So where can you find ideas that work for you? One sure technique for success in selling information is to look at what is making money for other people and let it make money for you, too. If you are fishing, you drop your line where the fish are biting. Do the same thing with your writing. Look at the subject of weight control, for instance. Is there just one successful book on the market? On the contrary, dozens are published every year. The key to success is not so much the originality of your subject as the originality, skill, and persistence with which you present and market it.

Utilize and build on the ideas and knowhow of others. Look at your friends and acquaintances with a new eye. What do they know that others would pay to know? I have a friend—a retired naval officer—who is setting himself up as a specialized nurseryman, growing and marketing a rare and much sought-after variety of English holly to florists nationwide. Another friend just completed a course of study at the local community college and now has his electrician's license and a three-truck business. A third acquaintance—a former high-level school administrator—has established a successful bed and breakfast hotel. Another friend, a more literary type, now runs a search service for rare books.

Would others want, need, and be able to profit from a handbook on how to do these and similar things themselves? Could you gather more success stories and combine them into a manual on home businesses for retired persons? The market for these products would be vast and growing: all of those retired people who are looking for sources of additional income as well as something interesting to do with their time.

Ideas from Newspapers and Magazines

Browse through four newspapers daily: your local paper, the newspaper of your state capital (or closest major metropolitan area), a national paper such as the *New York Times* or the *Washington Post*, and the *Wall Street Journal*. Look for trends, needs, products, research. I promise that once you start searching it will be a rare day that goes by without adding a couple of really strong book ideas to your inventory. Your only problem will be picking and choosing among them.

Do you see articles on a new (real) cure for baldness? An aid to male sexual potency? A hot business idea for retired persons? A piece on how to save money when buying a new car? These and many more could be packaged for mail-order information selling. You (or the writer to whom you assign the project) will simply write your source for more information, do some interviews, consult local specialists, read through other literature in the field, and put it all together in e-book form.

The Government Printing Office is a gold mine of information for mail-order sellers of information. For a catalog of government publications, write the Superintendent of Documents, Government Printing Office, Washington, DC 20402. Browse through the list and order the books that interest you. These are usually in the public domain (without protection of copyright), so you can use the information they contain in writing your own for-sale publications. Some examples? Opening the most recent Government Printing Office catalog to page 1, my eye falls on the title, "Fast Facts and Figures about Social Security." Combine this with information on Medicare and Medicaid (Medicare Handbook, page 8), other government programs for older Americans, plus additional tidbits derived from your own imagination and experience, and you can easily come up with a *Financial Fact Book for Retired Americans* that could promise everything you need to know about getting all the benefits you are entitled to during your retirement years.

On page 20 of the catalog is a blurb for a book called *Summary of Existing Legislation for Persons with Disabilities*. On page 26 is *Wise Home Buying* and on page 11, *Starting and Managing a Business from Your Home*. All such subjects can provide rich rewards to the desktop publisher selling information by mail.

You could develop a website called something like SurvivalSiteforSeniors.com to market these materials.

Building Your Website

I'm not going to tell you how to build your website. But here are three things to keep in mind:

1. I built mine, and knew nothing at all about how to do it when I started. What I did, you can do.
2. In website building, simpler is better. You are selling information. You just need to let the surfer know what you have to tell him, how it will help him, and how to get it.

3. There are books and tools to guide you through the process. I have recommended two of these on the last page of this chapter.

What You Say on Your Site

When you write the copy for your site you will use the same techniques that have been working for mail-order and direct-mail merchants for many years. Basically, effective copywriting is constructed according to the "AIDA" formula: attention, interest, desire, action.

1. Put the benefit to the customer up front. "How to Make $100,000 a Year in Desktop Publishing" and "How to Make Money Writing for Magazines" are two benefit-centered headlines I use. "Lose 30 Pounds a Month without Dieting" might be another. With your website you can experiment until you find the headline that produces the best results.
2. Explain how your product will deliver that benefit. This is the guts of your site, and must be colorful and complete. Mix in a strong element of desire. Help the reader visualize what life will be like with a bulging bank account or the most beautiful body on the beach.
3. Ask for the order and make ordering easy. Tell the reader how to take action to "make this dream a reality."
4. Seal the deal with a free trial period and a money-back guarantee.

I have not found a single book devoted specifically to copywriting for the web. Perhaps this is because there is very little to add to the several great ones already available on copywriting for mail-order ads. I am going to refer you to the best of them here. Study these books closely and use the tips they contain. They are derived from years of experience and are worthy of your confidence.

The first book I will recommend is possibly the finest book on advertising copywriting ever written. It is *Tested Advertising Methods*, by John Caples. Caples learned his trade in the mail-order business, so his advice is right on target. Another book that can help you achieve your goals of writing effective ad copy to sell books is Melvin Powers's *How I Made $1,000,000 in Mail Order*. Powers's book is especially interesting because his background is in mail-order book selling, specifically books that package information. He includes many reproductions of ads that have worked for him (and some that didn't work). These are lessons that you will put to work in developing your website. The third book is David Ogilvy's *Ogilvy on Advertising*. Pay particular attention to what he has to say about "irrelevant brilliance"—a trait that has led many web designers astray.

Getting the Money

One small hurdle. If you decide to sell your stuff from your own website, you will have to take payment via credit card. This may seem difficult if you have no experience with it, but it is really quite simple. Just go to your bank, tell them what you are doing, and ask them to help you set up a "merchant account."

If you have any problem with this, try another bank. Mine is through Bank of America. An associate has his through First Union. I have an electronic credit card terminal, bought through eBay, sitting beside my computer. When an order comes in, I type the credit card number into the machine, get instant approval, and the money is transferred into my bank account automatically. I have sold books and reports to buyers in countries all over the world in this simple way.

If you don't need a merchant account during the start-up phase and want to avoid the minimum monthly fee such an account entails, you can use a web-based service like ProPay or PayPal. These services are quite simple and quite usable, until the happy moment when the sheer volume of business forces you to do something else.

There are also online services like Cybercash or CCNow that will handle the entire transaction for you and simply transfer funds into your bank account once the sale is complete.

If You Build It, Will They Come?

Designing your site and even putting it up on the web is just the beginning. The trick is to get potential buyers to come there. Shari Thurow, in her fine book *Search Engine Visibility*, tells you clearly and directly what you must do to make your site one that search engines like Google and directories like Yahoo! will find worthy of listing.

Peter Kent reminds you to participate in mailing list discussion groups that cover your topic, to trade web links with other sites that appeal to your demographic base, to work the newsgroups on your topic, and to create an email signature file that promotes your site and your product.

But there are other things that Kent doesn't cover and that are perhaps most important of all: the promotion of your electronic business through print media products. Let's start with the classifieds.

The Secret: Attract Traffic with Classified Ads

Classified advertising is, without a doubt, the best buy in print media advertising today. Classified pages consistently pull more readers than any other section of the publication in which they appear. They are perfect for testing the salability of a new book idea and for testing alternate approaches and sales pitches to determine which pulls best.

Many of the very best magazines have classified sections, and almost all trade magazines—those with specialized readerships—do. There is affordable mass media classified advertising in publications like the *National Enquirer*, read by millions of people each week. There is specialized mass media advertising in such newspapers as the *Wall Street Journal*, which even has regional buys available. And there are the magazines that go to reasonably well-defined and targeted readerships, such as *Writer's Digest, The Writer,* and scores of others.

I am in the process of placing some classifieds now. Since I don't have to do the whole selling job in the ads themselves I can usually fit my ads within the minimum word category for the publication I want to advertise in. All you need to do is use a strong lead to get readers to go to your website for details.

Here is an ad that I am placing in the classified pages of *Writer's Digest*:

Start Your Own Magazine with
No Cash Up Front.
Details at www.PubMart.com.

I am also placing an ad in *Entrepreneur*:

Make Big Bucks Publishing Your Own
City Magazines and Tabloids. No cost,
no risk start-up. Details at
www.PubMart.com.

Look through the magazines at your library or on the racks at the biggest newsstand nearby. Which ones are likely to attract readers interested in your niche-market information products? Do these magazines have classified sections? Are there other ads selling information? Do they appear issue after issue? If the answer to these questions is yes, then that newspaper or magazine may be worth a try.

Inventory the publications that seem likely to reach your market. In the reference rooms of most libraries you will find standard references such as *Gebbie's All-In-One Directory*.

Advertising in specialized magazines can be valuable to the information seller, since there is no waste circulation. You can carefully target the reader interest group or groups that you want to reach. Those who get the magazines are pre-qualified. Everyone who reads *Publishers Weekly*, for instance, is likely to be interested in books and publishing. Readers of *American Firefighter* are surely interested in fire-fighting equipment and supplies and the personal welfare of firemen. In addition you will want to consider general circulation publications like *National Enquirer*. Its hundreds of thousands of readers will respond to ads for books on making money, losing weight, and other topics of more general interest.

When you single out a publication that you are interested in, study the demographic profile of its readership as carefully as possible. Are these the people you want to reach? Check out the advertising rates and measure investment against probable and possible return.

You can get the telephone number and address of advertising sales offices by looking at the information given on the masthead. Or you can obtain it from Gebbie's directory or from a reference publication like *Standard Rate and Data Service*. Write or call requesting that you be sent a media kit containing all rates, specifically classified (words only) and classified display (words and design) rates, and demographic information on the readership. You will have these in hand quite quickly. The media kit will also contain a sample copy of the publication for your files.

Standard Rate and Data Service (SRDS), available at most large libraries, contains circulation and advertising rate information, but usually not in as much detail as the media kit. On the other hand it will be far more objective in the presentation of its data, whereas the media kit is essentially a sales piece.

Write Articles Promoting Your Products

As a writer you can create and publish magazine articles that give your website a boost. Shortly after I put my site up on the web I wrote an article for *Publishing for Entrepreneurs* magazine that di-

Hometown

HOW-TO

America's
Kitchen Table
Publisher

**Opportunities in Entrepreneurial Publishing:
What They Are and Where to Find Them**

This is the opening spread for my article on publishing city and regional magazines and newspapers that appeared in *Publishing for Entrepreneurs* magazine. It directed scores of readers directly to my website, where many of them bought my products. Such articles can bring great visibility to you and your site.

rectly touted the information products I was selling on the web. I sold the article to the magazine at a bargain basement price because I knew that the publicity it would give me was much more valuable. I was right. *Publishing for Entrepreneurs* magazine featured my article on the cover, gave it a lead position in the magazine, and included an "about the author" write-up that directed readers to my website. You can't get better than that. As a freelance writer, you can easily develop article ideas that when written and published will help build traffic on your site.

Other Web Sales Opportunities

There are other web sales opportunities for your writing. Some websites will pay you to write articles (in web parlance, "create content") for them but at present none offers a decent fee for the work you perform. I gave the Writer-on-Line site a crack a while back, but the $25 to $50 per article fee they offered at that time was laughable. You will want to do this kind of writing only in return for promotion for your own website.

Sites like the old MightyWords.com will sell your articles for you and take a percentage as their cut. There are a few others out there now, and you can track them down through Google. Sites like Booklocker.com will sell e-book versions of your books and booklets, taking a percentage for their services. POD publishers like XLibris and IUniverse will publish your book for you at a reasonable charge. However, with all of these options you still have the problem of publicizing your work and giving it the visibility that will attract buyers. You are far better off marketing your work on your own site, where you remain in charge of the whole process and, when successful, reap all the rewards.

Your Internet Tool Kit

Here's what you will need to start building your site:

1. A good manual. I recommend Peter Kent's *Poor Richard's Web Site* and *Search Engine Visibility*, by Shari Thurow.
2. A list of the best sites that sell products similar to yours and in ways that will be similar to yours. You will study these sites to glean ideas for your own. Take the best and discard the rest.
3. A site plan. You can draw this out on paper or use a page layout program like Adobe PageMaker. Do this just as you would if you were designing a print media ad, complete with headlines and copy.
4. A web editing program. I use Adobe GoLive and Dreamweaver. One of the stand-bys is FrontPage, by Microsoft, but many complain about the way FrontPage manipulates the HTML code.

— 11 —

Business Details: Rights and Contracts

WHEN A PUBLICATION ACCEPTS your query it will send you some kind of contractual agreement (often called an "assignment letter") that specifies the topic and length of the article they expect you to write, establishes a deadline for delivery and names the fee that they will pay for it. These agreements can range from quite simple in the case of local or small regional magazines to somewhat more complex in the case of publications with larger circulation or when a wider range of rights is at issue.

As a professional writer you must understand that this contract is a binding document that will define the uses that the purchasing publication can make of your work as well as the money you are going to earn. If you see terms and conditions that you don't like, don't hesitate to call the editor you are dealing with and try to negotiate a deal that is more to your liking. Often the contract you have been sent is simply a standard one, and the editor will be glad to modify it. In other cases it is pretty much written in stone, and you take it or leave it. In either case remember that the contract attorneys for the magazine wrote the contract and it is full of clauses that protect the magazine but do not do much to protect you.

The Rights You Are Selling

When you "sell" an article to a magazine or other periodical— unless you sell "all rights" or write your piece as a "work made for hire" (see below)—you are in reality not selling but licensing your article for a particular use. You don't want to give away more than is necessary to make the deal. Here are some of the terms and conditions you should understand with respect to the licensing of rights:

- *All rights.* When you license all rights you give up ownership rights to your article totally and completely. Some magazines routinely specify "all rights" in their freelance agreements but may be quite willing to negotiate a wording more favorable to the writer.

- *First serial rights.* When you license first serial rights you give the publishing magazine the right to print your article before anyone else does, but you retain the right to use it later in other ways—in a book, for instance. A version of my article, "The Freelancer's Paradigm," appeared in *Writer's Journal* magazine under a grant of first serial rights. It was later sold to *Writers Online*. Parts of it also appear in this book. If I had sold all rights instead of first serial rights to *Writer's Journal*, I would not have been free to use the work in any of these other ways.

- *First North American print serial rights.* When you license first North American serial rights, you grant the publishing magazine the right to print your article before anyone else in North America alone, keeping resale rights to other English-speaking markets and translation rights in the foreign language markets for yourself.

- *Work made for hire.* The phrase "work made for hire" appears in the current copyright law. Here's what it means. When a writer agrees that the manuscript he is producing is a work made for hire, he is giving up all rights to his literary product. The person, magazine, or publisher who commissions the work and pays you for it owns it outright. The writer is simply the person they have hired to produce it for them. If you do enter into such an agreement, your compensation ought to be quite a bit higher than for a simple first rights agreement.

- *Archival rights and electronic reproduction rights.* The magazine that publishes your work may want to post it in an online version of their publication, or it may even "relicense" the article for archiving on an online database or for other electronic use. Electronic rights are getting to be big business these days, and the rules of the game are not yet firmly established. Don't agree to license such rights without getting some compensation for them. You have to protect yourself. When the original publisher finds another income-producing outlet for your work, you should be contacted and additional compensation negotiated. Not so long ago it was enough to specify "first serial rights" or "first North American serial rights" without adding the word "print" to the mix. No more. You want to make it clear that you retain electronic rights. I add the words "excludes all electronic rights" to my agreements to make this even clearer. If the publisher objects, and if you still want to do the deal (as most of us do), then suggest some enhancement of your writer's fee for the grant of electronic rights. If a magazine offers you $1,000 for the article, suggest $1,000-plus (I leave the details to you) for the bigger package. If you are a beginner and can't negotiate a better deal, you may want to accept whatever terms are offered for the sake of building your portfolio of clips, but don't be pressured into doing this before you have to. These are murky areas indeed, since the onset of electronic dissemination of information has been so sudden that no consensus on rights and compensation has yet developed.

Read your assignment letter carefully and measure it against this list of issues. Limit the rights you are assigning to the publisher to the degree that you can do so. Traditionally, an author specifies the rights that he is offering for sale in the upper right-hand corner of the first page of the manuscript, along with the number of words in the article.

Check Out This Source of Information: NWU

You will find a great deal of useful information on the sale of rights on the National Writers Union website (www.nwu.com). As I write this I have just visited their site and found the following list of publications the Union offers to freelancers:

- *Authors in the New Information Age: Electronic Publishing Issues*
- *Standard Journalism Contracts and Handbook*
- *NWU Guide to Book Contracts*
- *NWU Guide and Model Contract for Ghostwriting & Collaborations*
- *NWU Preferred Literary Agent Agreement and Understanding the Agent-Author Relationship*
- *NWU Guide to Fair Use*
- *Electronic Rights Policy*
- *Electronic Rights Negotiation Strategies*
- *Statement of Principles on Electronic Books*
- *Recommended Principles for Contracts Covering Online Book Publishing*
- *Technical Writers Code of Practice (Hardware/Software Industries)*

ASJA on Electronic Rights

The American Society of Journalists and Authors has some excellent articles on the subject of electronic rights on its web site at www.shsl.com/93.htm. It will be well worth your while to go there and read them.

Your Compensation

You will quickly discover that the publishing business thrives on the backs of the people who write for it. This includes newspaper reporters, freelance writers, and all but the most successful book authors. That's a fact. Unless you are very talented, very lucky, a superb promoter—or all three—you are not likely to get rich. Still, you can earn very welcome and substantial amounts of money by writing. And if you don't think that luck and promotion form the greater part of the package, consider the success of such books as the *Chicken Soup for the Soul* series or *The Celestine Prophecy.* Certainly, raw literary talent was not part of the mix.

By the Word or by the Piece

Some publications offer payment by the word and some by the article. But even when the price is set for the article as a whole, a length has always been specified by the publisher and the length of the piece still comes into the picture. The range of payment varies widely, from a low of a few hundred dollars to a ceiling of $3,000 to $4,000—and sometimes more for really dramatic, exclusive pieces.

Only the top writers with the most powerful bylines can expect to get top dollar from top publications. Most freelancers earn from $500 to $2,000 per article. The more often you write for a magazine the more you will make. And when editors come to you with a project assignment, you will do better yet.

"On Spec" Assignments

From time to time, especially in the beginning, you will be offered an "on spec" assignment. Editors will offer on spec assignments when they like an idea but are not familiar with your work and don't know if you can write the article in a way that suits their editorial style and format. I accepted many on spec assignments when I was getting started, but almost never do now.

An editor has no obligation to buy an on spec article once you finish it and submit it but he is clearly letting you know that if you do a good job he will most likely do so. You may ask for a "kill fee" (see the next section), but such fees are not usually granted in the case of on spec submissions.

The Kill Fee

Sometimes the contract that the publisher offers will specify that a kill fee may be paid to the author for a finished article in lieu of publication and full compensation. When a kill fee is paid, all rights to the article revert to the author and he or she is free to place it elsewhere.

Why would a publisher kill an article that has been written under contract? Many reasons. Perhaps the editorial format of the magazine has changed since the article was assigned. Perhaps the purchasing editor has moved to another job. Perhaps events have made the article untimely.

For whatever reason, if this clause is in the contract, the publisher has the right to exercise it and decline to publish your article. But if he does, he must pay you the kill fee you have agreed upon.

You can sometimes negotiate the amount to be paid in the event of non-publication. Some kill fees are set at 25 percent of the agreed writer's fee. This is very low and not very fair to the writer. After all, the article was written for a particular magazine in a particular style. Much work will be required to rewrite it even if another buyer can be found. Further, a low kill fee makes it too easy for the magazine to walk away from a project with relative impunity. Always try to negotiate a kill fee of 50 percent or better.

Be Careful What Warranties You Give

There will be a clause in most contracts in which you, as author, warrant that the submitted article is free of plagiarism and that it has not appeared elsewhere. All of that is fine and to be expected.

You should refuse, however, to sign an agreement which asks

you to warrant that the article is free of libel or other actionable elements. You are not a lawyer. Keep this particular monkey on the publisher's back, where it belongs. Don't let it jump over to yours. It is the publisher's job to submit articles to one of its staff attorneys to get final clearance.

You may also be asked to hold the publisher "harmless" (not liable) for the costs of any lawsuit resulting from the publication of your article. Such a clause makes you responsible for paying the legal fees yourself. "Hold harmless" agreements are very dangerous for you. Nuisance lawsuits may be filed which the plaintiff has no hope of winning but which nevertheless can clean out the defendant's bank account and everything else he owns. Can you pay those big bucks? Do not accept such a clause in your agreement. Legal fees are the publisher's responsibility, not yours.

Copyright Your Work

Should you take the trouble to copyright your articles? Yes, you should. Piracy of intellectual property (your writing) is more widespread than ever before due to the rapidly increasing number of so-called "content sites" on the Internet. This doesn't mean that there is a thief behind every bush or that editors in general are out to steal your ideas. Such beliefs—paranoia, even—can cripple a writer's ability to function in the freelance marketplace. Nevertheless, as long as there is no law on the Internet frontier you must take steps to protect yourself until such time as the sheriff arrives and Internetland settles down to become a civil society of law-abiding citizens. Here are some things you should know:

- Under the current copyright law, you own the copyright to your work from the moment of creation, whether or not it is registered. However, if you ever have to prove the date that you actually wrote your piece you will be handicapped without the copyright registration certificate in hand.

- A magazine usually has a notice of copyright on the masthead page. However, this copyright applies only to the magazine as a collective work and not to the individual articles it contains. These must be registered individually by their authors.
- Though you technically own the copyright interests in your work, published or unpublished, from the moment of creation, you cannot sue for infringement of copyright until the allegedly infringed work is registered.
- To register your copyright and obtain your certificate, follow these instructions: To obtain copies of forms TX and GR/GP call the U.S. Copyright office. Phone: (202) 707-3000, 8:30-5:00 Eastern time, Monday-Friday. Use form TX to register one or more unpublished manuscripts. These can be grouped to avoid having to file a separate application for each work and to avoid having to pay a $30 registration fee for each work. Detailed instructions are provided on the ASJA website.
- Get a rubber stamp from your office supply store. Have the following line set in ten point type: *Copyright (Year) by (Your Name).* Stamp tear sheets, reprints, and copies that you distribute for publicity, promotion, or any other purpose. This is not strictly necessary in a legal sense, but it may help prevent problems of unwitting copyright infringement.

— 12 —

Writing for Businesses

I AM A WRITER and a book publisher. Recently a nearby university asked me to design a new magazine for their school. I did so and earned several thousand dollars. Designing magazines is not my major source of income. Writing and publishing is. But when the opportunity came to pick up this extra chunk of cash, I was glad to accept it.

There have been other such assignments. Some time ago a young entrepreneur asked me to write a franchise manual for the chain of restaurants he was setting up. I went to the library to find out what was in a franchise manual, signed an agreement with him, and collected a $5,000 fee, far more than I could have earned from any magazine article I might have written.

While I was writing for and publishing regional magazines, I was asked to develop a sixteen-page image-enhancing publication for a five-county consortium in my part of the state. This contract brought in another four-figure fee. These were lucrative *secondary profit centers*. Secondary profit centers will come your way, too, once you become known as a writer. These can be very important to you as you work to build income from your freelance writing. The following sections outline just a few of the typical opportunities that may come your way.

Capabilities Brochures

With the capabilities brochure we get into the higher levels of income potential from secondary profit centers. Such a project gives you the opportunity to make money in several ways. You can profit from writing, from design, and from brokering the printing of the job.

A capabilities brochure is a company's chief sales piece, and it must be very well done. The customer is usually willing to pay whatever it takes to get the job done right. He is not, however, interested in wasting money. The advertising agencies that will compete for such jobs are likely to be much more expensive than you are. You can do a 100 percent markup and still be competitive. Agencies typically have a much higher overhead than you will have, and they will be staffed with highly paid graphic artists. You will be using freelancers for the most part, and you do not have to maintain the expensive image in your offices that the ad agency does.

For the agency, remember, such brochures represent primary rather than secondary profit centers. They have much less room to play around with pricing, since they have to factor a major portion of their overhead into their quotes on such work. Your own overhead is covered by your publishing business. I am talking about full-fledged, multi-page capabilities brochures. The small, three-panel jobs will not be profitable for you, and your prices will not be competitive. Any print shop can, and will, throw one of these together at rock-bottom prices, often including the (admittedly unimaginative) design work into the bargain at no charge. Stay away from these. They bring too much grief for too little money.

Once you have assembled the necessary talent—whether freelance or in-house—you can begin to keep an eye out for work designing and producing product catalogs for your clients. Product catalogs are photography and design intensive, and the printing is likely to be expensive. You will be dealing with a considerable sum of money, so no matter what your percentage of markup you are likely to make a good profit on the job. Another nice thing about such jobs is that they tend to be repeated. If you do a good job at a competitive price this year, the client will come to you again next year for an update.

Sometimes you will get requests to reprint the very same catalog.

Annual Reports

Corporations that are publicly traded must prepare annual reports for their shareholders. These reports are typically showpieces of design and printing. If the shareholders knew how much the report actually cost them, they might decide to instruct management to send out photocopied sheets with the same information on them.

But, happily for you, they do not do this, and the fancy, expensive annual report has become a fixture in American business. Your clients will be those corporations that are large enough to require an annual report but small enough that they do not have an ad agency or a public relations firm on retainer.

There are many such firms. Local and regional banks and savings and loan institutions are excellent prospects. Your proposal will have to be made to the corporate headquarters. If you live on the East Coast and discover that the corporate headquarters of the business in question is in Los Angeles, then you cannot service that prospect. In the area where I ran one of my former companies, the giant, multinational drug manufacturing firm Glaxo has its American headquarters nearby. But it was too large a company for my small firm to approach successfully. On the other hand, a new regional chain of banks had just begun to do business. This was a prime candidate for my company. So is the small plastics-manufacturing firm that has set up shop in the industrial park nearby, and there are many others.

How much time do you spend prospecting such potential customers? I find that a daily phone call or two to purchasing agents or others in charge of getting the reports, catalogs, and capabilities brochures done, will land an opportunity to make a proposal and generate as much of this kind of work as I can handle. If you find that you are really good at getting this kind of business and producing documents that please your clients, you can profitably spend more and more time doing it. It could in time move up from a secondary to primary profit center or become the nucleus of a separate business.

Operations Manuals

Owners and managers require many documents that they cannot generate in-house. Usually a limited number of copies is needed, so printing is not an important factor in the cost. It is the writing and desktop design services that you will provide.

A short time ago a young entrepreneur came to my office. He had developed an idea for a chain of fast-food restaurants that he would place in shopping malls throughout the region. To franchise his idea he had to develop a complete operations manual. He asked if we could help, and we immediately said that we could.

The entrepreneur, whom I will call Stan, was not a writer. It is doubtful if he had ever even written a long letter. But he was a man of action and knew the fast-food business from top to bottom. Since Stan could not generate even a rough draft of his ideas for me to revise, I took another approach. I interviewed him and got everything down on tape. Some sections he dictated into my recorder while driving from one of his business locations to another. I transcribed all of this material and edited it.

This constituted the first rough draft. I then gave it to Stan for revision. He dictated new passages, filled in the blanks, and we followed the same process through again. After we had a second draft, I asked him to have his operations manager, his attorney, and his accountant read through the manual and add their own notes. Their observations were noted and their additions duly incorporated into the text. I then generated a final proof copy. After we corrected the typos and made a few minor textual changes, this became the final version.

Stan signed the authorization-to-print form that I always use, and I printed the operations manual and had it bound in looseleaf form so that later additions and changes could be made easily. There were just fifty copies. Since I am a writer and had time to take it on, I did the manual myself. Had I not been a writer, I could easily have assigned it to a freelancer.

My profit on this job, after all expenses, was several thousand dollars. In a major metropolitan area I would have made much more than that, but of course my overhead would have been much greater and my chances of getting the job reduced because of the more competitive environment.

Business Plans

The business plan is a key document for any business, especially any new business. The care and professionalism with which it is written and designed will favorably influence the decisions of bankers and others important to the financial success of the enterprise.

The business plan is also important to the entrepreneur himself, since it is his own map of the commercial terrain he intends to conquer and his guidebook to the way he does business. I have developed many business plans over the years for my own businesses, so I have learned what the elements of a good one are. When developing a business plan for a client, I often use the same interview method that I used with Stan and his fast-food franchise. I simply ask the appropriate questions and help the client work through his ideas to develop good answers. I am not a lawyer, so I steer clear of giving hard legal advice. But I do get the facts down in such a way that they become clear to any interested reader.

From time to time I would insert house ads in one of my own magazines offering a business plan service. Each time I placed the ad I drew a couple of responses from entrepreneurs who became paying clients. Many of these people are under-financed, so you cannot always get top dollar for your work. Nevertheless, it is a profitable sideline, a financial gap-filler.

Work with Accountants

Another approach is to work with accountants. You call on them, make them aware of your capabilities, and ask for the opportunity to do the business plans (and annual reports) of their clients for them. Often they will be very happy to farm their work out, and they pay well for it. The accountant deals with the customer, you deal only with the accountant. As a result you know from the very beginning precisely what is to be included in the plan, and you are furnished with raw copy that is usually in pretty fair form. You simply edit this material; design the financial tables, graphs, spreadsheets, etc.; and provide the accountant with the necessary number of copies.

Employee Manuals

There comes a time when every growing business needs an employee and operations manual. For larger enterprises these are separate documents, but for smaller businesses they are easily combined. My own company uses the combined version. In the first months we simply communicated our company policies, procedures, and benefits to each new person individually. Soon, however, this was no longer sufficient. We were still a very small firm by any standard. I did not always see everyone every day. I needed a written statement of what I offered my employees and what I expected from them.

An employee manual is very simple to do. You can prepare a questionnaire for your client and put together the manual by collating and rewriting his answers to your questions. There are many good books on this subject that will provide an outline for you. The Small Business Administration (SBA) offers one for free.

Seminars

If you have a flair for speaking and think well on your feet, you can put together a menu of two- or three-hour seminars that you can present on your own or under the auspices of your chamber of commerce, community college, or the SBA. The seminars you give will grow out of your background and abilities. Sample topics might be such subjects as "How to Publish Your Book"; "How to Make Money Writing"; "How to Write an Employee Manual"; "How to Position Your Product or Service in the Marketplace"; "How to Design and Publish a Company Newsletter or Magazine"; and many others in the same vein. It all depends on what you know and can talk about.

You can profit from these seminars in two ways. First of all, you get paid the usual fee as seminar presenter. In addition, you make contact with business people who are impressed by your knowledge of the subject and unsure of their own, and who will contract with you to prepare the materials they need.

Editing and Ghost Writing

This kind of work just appears on your doorstep from time to time. There is usually not much you can do to attract it. I have done this work profitably, although it was often more time-consuming than I anticipated. You have to be careful to deal only with those who can afford your services. I ghosted an "autobiography" for which I had a wonderful collection of memoirs, diaries, and letters to draw upon. My subject was a good natural writer, and this helped. I set the fee at $10,000. Based on the time it took, I should have asked $20,000 or more. On shorter jobs I generally will work for $75 an hour. The client usually wants a firm price, so I estimate how long it will take and multiply that figure by my hourly rate. Ghost writing requires concentrated effort and attention. To try to do it at a fire-sale rate is neither possible nor profitable.

I occasionally send a mailing piece to CEOs and purchasing agents in my area, advertising my services as a publications consultant. I also find it worthwhile to advertise these services in the pages of the more prestigious magazines. As a consultant I help business, government, and industrial clients develop publications that attain the goals set for them. I develop editorial formats and physical formats. I show them how to write, edit, lay out, and print their publications. I help them set up schedules and procedures that assure a timely, quality product. All of these services are very valuable, and I find that whenever a client who needs my services comes my way he is generally willing to pay a reasonable price for them.

Financial understandings with your secondary profit center activities should be made quite clear, otherwise you risk trouble. Verbal agreements are easily misinterpreted. Ambiguity has no place in a financial transaction. You need a written agreement signed by you and by your client specifying precisely what goods and services you agree to deliver and what sum of money your client agrees to pay for them, and how and when payment is due.

Build your reputation as a writer. It is a marketable commodity in your own community.

— 13 —

How to Build Your Reputation as a Writer

WHILE THERE ARE EXCEPTIONS to every generalization, you can count on there being few reputations in any field that are not self-made. Don't expect on the good fairy to do things for you that you are unwilling to do for yourself. The good fairy is notoriously unreliable, and will seldom take time to fulfill your basic needs, much less your fondest expectations. The personal, professional, and even financial rewards that will come to the writer who sees to his own publicity are substantial indeed.

As a writer you and you alone are the chief marketer of your wares. This chore is not unique to writers. It is well known in the publishing industry that, except for very rare exceptions, only hard promotional work on the part of the writer will keep even the most potentially saleable articles and books on the market long enough to become successful.

Dr. Wayne Dyer did that when he loaded case after case of *Your Erroneous Zones* into the trunk of his car and took off on a self-sponsored, cross-country tour. James Redfield sold *The Celestine Prophecy* on his own for many months before it was picked by Time-Warner and hit the big time. While article writers are not dealing with such big bucks, and while blockbuster commercial success is almost certainly out of their reach, their self-promotional efforts are just as essential to their success, or even more so.

Prepare a Media Kit

The first step is to prepare a media kit. These used to be called "press kits," as though television didn't exist, but no more. The media kit is your most important information packet, and it is designed to make the work of those from whom you hope to get coverage that much easier.

Each item in it will have multiple uses. Sometimes you will send the complete kit. Sometimes you will send only the news release or some other single item.

A complete media kit will contain the following items:

- A fact sheet on yourself as author. This fact sheet will include a short bio of you, a listing of your credits, short excerpts from favorable reviews or interviews (if you have written a book), a statement of your goals and motivations as a writer, irresistible quotes, etc. Keep it in easily utilized, outline form so that a feature writer or reporter can find and excerpt materials that are needed for a write-up.

  In preparing this fact sheet, as in preparing all the other marketing materials in your repertoire, bear in mind that reporters—whether print or electronic—will not have time to research an article on you and your work. You have to do this for them. When your fact sheet is well done and easily utilized you take a giant step toward getting the kind of publicity you need. The fact sheet can also be used as a background piece to include in your submissions to magazines and to book publishers. It can be given to program chairmen who have to introduce you to audiences before whom you are scheduled to appear. You can have it blown up to poster size and use it as a prop at readings, autograph parties, and other occasions.
- A fact sheet on your specialty or specialties.
- Clips of major articles that you have had published. You will photocopy these and keep them readily available.

- Copies of any other articles that have been written about you.
- A brief news release of one full page or less—a short, straightforward story telling about your latest publishing credit.
- A complete feature article of 500 to 700 words, with photographs. This piece is a personality profile of you and your work. Will the article be used? Sometimes it will and sometimes it won't. It all depends on the space availability and intrinsic interest of your article. *One thing, though, is certain. It will not be used if you do not write it and send it out.* Some newspapers—especially weeklies, which will be happy to have a free feature—will print it just as you provide it.
- Include a glossy, black-and-white photograph of yourself. Some kind of action shot in a natural surrounding will get better play than a simple mug shot since it will have greater reader interest. If you are writing a poem about your conquest of Mount Everest, the photograph ought to show you on the summit.

Small but Powerful Publications

Do not overlook association newsletters, organizational magazines, and other second-line publications. These can be a great help in creating the kind of public recognition you need. If there are other tie-ins, be sure to exploit them. If your article commemorates some historical occasion, for instance, and you are a member of the local historical society, send a package to the organization's magazine or newsletter editor. If you are a member of the American Legion and your writing has a patriotic theme, send a copy to *American Legion Magazine.* You won't hit many of the national publications at the right time, and you will have to understand that the competition for limited space is fierce. But take advantage of every possibility. You will not get your message into print every time you attempt to do so, but when you succeed the results can be very important to you. You can ask to have a copy of any review sent to you, but normally this is not done. You will not know of reviews in papers you don't regularly read until some acquaintance tells you, casually, "Hey, I read about you in the paper last week."

Bombard the World with News Releases

You will not want to send your complete media kit to everyone. It is too expensive. But you should send a news release to every possible source of publicity.

Do news releases work? You bet they do. Some time back I organized a small publishing company to bring out a commercial magazine. Everything worked fine, except for one thing. Since I was new in business, the printer wanted to be paid in advance. I could not collect from my advertisers until I had the published magazine in hand. Where was I going to get the $20,000 I needed to pay the printing bill?

I went to the banks. They liked what I was doing but politely pointed out that I had no track record. I thought about this response and realized that these bankers had never heard of me or my company before. I set about to remedy that. I sent small news releases out weekly. My company was bringing out this new magazine or that, expanding its operations into this area or that, hiring this person or that as vice-president for sales (vice-presidents get into print more easily than sales managers), and every other positive thing that could possibly be imagined. I concluded each short release with a paragraph about my position as president and my own credentials.

After three months I approached a new bank. "Yes," the banker said, "I've been reading about you and your company. How can I help?" And in short order I had the line of credit I needed. I was the same. My company was the same. I had merely increased my positive public visibility through the effective use of news releases.

A news release is not a feature story. It tells, in the terse style of straight news stories, the facts of your book and its publication. The best releases will be one page in length. This length is manageable and fits easily into filler space in newspapers. In no case should your release run more than a page and a half unless there is something far more newsworthy involved than the mere fact that you have written and published a book.

The shorter and more concise the news release, the more likely it is to be picked up by newspapers. News releases must fit available space. This means that editors often lop off a final paragraph or two when they put your release in place. Since you know that this often happens you will get all the essential information in the first few paragraphs. The closing portion, while containing readable information, will be expendable. The release will stand alone with or without it.

Always write your release in newspaper style. If you don't, no one will have time to rewrite it, and it will be discarded.

A Release for Every Occasion

When should you send out news releases? There are more occasions than you might imagine. Remember that your goal is not only to sell a particular book but to build your reputation as a writer and literary figure of importance.

Here are some typical occasions that merit news releases:

- You publish an article in a magazine of note.
- You publish a book. Send a separate release on acceptance and another on publication.
- You give a talk to a club.
- You are elected to an office in an arts organization.

How to Get on Television

There are several steps to getting on television. You can succeed, but you may have to throw out several lines to catch a single fish.

(This short news release announces an award made to a poet, and at the same time plugs the poet's latest book. It is concise and easy for the editor to use. Type the words "LOCAL ANGLE" on the front of the envelope to alert the editor that the release concerns someone or something of local interest.)

John Doe
111 South Muse Place
Artsville, NC 12345

FOR IMMEDIATE RELEASE

Artsville Poet Honored

Artsville poet John Doe has been named winner of the North Carolina Society of Poetry award for best poem on a North Carolina theme for 1991.

In making the award, Marvin Major, president of the Society, singled out Doe's "deep understanding of the values we all cherish: home, family and community."

Doe's verse has previously appeared in national and regional publications. He is also author of the recently published book, Scenes of the Outer Banks. Doe is a member of the Artsville Council for the Arts, and secretary of the creative writing division of the North Carolina Literature Coalition.

-End-

Note to the editor: The enclosed poem may be reproduced "by permission of John Doe. Copyright by John Doe, 2000." Review copies of Scenes of the Outer Banks may be obtained by calling the telephone number at the top of this release. John Doe is available for interview on topics of literary and artistic interest to the community.

Your first move is to send out a television news release. This varies somewhat from a print media news release, but it conveys the same basic information.

- Include a routing box on your television news release as follows:

> **Routing:**
> ❏ *News Director*
> ❏ *Lifestyle*
> ❏ *Talk show hosts*

- Double and triple up on your television contacts. Your news release should be beefed up with your complete media kit, sent to talk-show hosts by name, and reinforced by telephone calls to the same individuals.
- Send out "available-for-interview" flyers to talk-show hosts. These sheets are designed to tell them, at a glance, why you will be a good interview. This is worth some effort, as it is good business to be seen on local and regional talk shows. These shows are constantly on the lookout for anybody doing anything interesting and you, as a published writer, can fill that bill, as long as you let them know just why what you have to say will be interesting. This sheet will include your photo, your brief bio, a section telling what your book is about, and, most important, a section suggesting strong viewer-pulling topics, e.g., "How to unlock the creative force within."
- Give them the double whammy. Call them directly *and* send them an available-for-interview sheet.
- A tip: no-shows are a constant problem on local talk shows. When you speak to the talk-show hosts let them know that you are available on short notice and can fill in for last minute cancellations—a sure way to get your good-looking profile on camera in short order.

(Your "Available for Interview" form tells why you will be an interesting and entertaining guest. It includes your photograph, credentials, and a list of topics you are prepared to talk about, expressed in viewer-centered language. Here, in abbreviated form, is an <u>Available for Interview</u> form that I might invent for this book on publishing poetry.)

AVAILABLE FOR INTERVIEW

Your photo here

Tom Williams, Ph.D., is the author of the best-selling book, *Poet Power: The Complete Guide to Getting Your Poetry Published.* Williams is also the author of *Tales of the Tobacco Country*, a collection of history and folklore; *How to Make $100,000 a Year in Desktop Publishing*; and *Breaking Free: How to Win Financial Freedom Through Your Home-based Business.* He is President of Venture Press, a book publishing company based in Savannah, GA, and is a former editor and publisher of *Tar Heel: The Magazine of North Carolina.*

Thousands of everyday people are starved for creative expression. Dr. Williams's ideas and encouragement tell them how to release their innate creative power in their own lives.

On your show, Dr. Williams will talk about such topics as:

• How to unlock the hidden wells of creativity within.

• How to find and explore your secret *idea-center*.

• Nine secrets of publishable poetry.

• How to find hundreds of little-known magazines that will publish your poems.

• How to write, publish, and sell a book of your own poems.

Tom Williams will be available in your area on: _____

Dr. Tom Williams
Address
Contact Information

The Payoff

There is more than one way to make money freelancing. If you take the work of self-promotion seriously you will find that profit can flow in from unexpected sources. If you are a teacher, for instance, your journalistic credits can help put you first in line when raise and promotion time comes around. One early publication of mine brought in just $280 in royalties, but got me promoted to associate professor with a hefty increase in salary. Indirectly, I figure, I earned more than $100,000 over the years from that one source.

There will be payoff for the ego too. As you become recognized by your peers as a published writer, you will be invited to appear on panels, participate in discussion groups, and appear at writer's conferences, and be appointed to arts council assignments.

Appendix I
Contacts and Sources

Books

The books listed below are few in number but very solid in content. Each of them has been a valuable source of information and inspiration for me in setting up and managing my publishing businesses. Each contains concrete, usable information and techniques that can make you money. I highly recommend them to you. Since many of these books exist in a variety of editions, some expensive and some much less expensive, I suggest that you consult *Books in Print* and *Paperback Books in Print* at your library or bookstore to find the one that best fits your needs and pocketbook.

AP Stylebook and Libel Manual. Almost everything you need to know about newspaper style is contained in this book. It can become a valuable manual which sets specific style standards for all your publications. It is inexpensive and can be furnished to everyone in your editorial department.

Balkin, Richard. A *Writer's Guide to Book Publishing*. Written from the writer's perspective, Balkin's book is a primer on the business side of publishing. There is a useful and thorough discussion of book publishing contracts.

Capon, Rene J. *Associated Press Guide to News Writing: A Handbook for Writers*. An extremely useful, valuable guide to journalistic style, and not just for newspaper writers. All very practical, usable tips. The coverage of what not to do will save even experienced writers from making embarrassing gaffes, especially when writing for newspapers.

The Chicago Manual of Style. University of Chicago Press. This utterly complete handbook is as close to an industry standard as any. It should be on every writer's bookshelf. Academic (scholarly) writers may prefer the *Modern Language Association Stylebook*, and social scientists sometimes prefer the *American Psychological Association Stylebook*. The Chicago manual is the big one, and the most generally accepted.

Feldman, Elaine. *The Writer's Guide to Self Promotion & Publicity*. Writer's Digest Books. Publishing companies have "publicists" who promote their books for them. These days, however, many writers find they have to promote their own books and be their own publicists. This book tells how it can be done.

Fletcher, Tana, and Julia Rockler. *Getting Publicity: A Do-it-Yourself Guide for Small Business and Non Profit Groups*. Self Counsel Press. Good on tips for those in literary publishing and the arts.

Glenn, Peggy. *Publicity for Books and Authors: A Do-It-Yourself Handbook for Small Publishing Firms and Enterprising Authors*. Aames Allen Publishing Co. I found Peggy Glenn especially helpful in her chapters on dealing with radio and TV public relations and promotion.

Haldeman-Julius, Emmanuel. *The First Hundred Million*. Newspaperman-publisher Haldeman-Julius tells the fascinating story of the creation of his "Little Blue Book" series. The Blue Books were simple, saddle-stitched pamphlets containing reprints of the classics as well as practical information on such then-taboo topics as sex education for women. Everyone interested in the publishing and book world should treat themselves to a read of this book. There is a great chapter on the "Book Hospital" to which he consigned titles that were not selling well, tinkered with the title, and transformed them into profitable publications. If you think the choice of a title is unimportant, this chapter will change your mind. This chapter is also available on my website at www.PubMart.com.

Henderson, Bill. *The Publish-It-Yourself Handbook*. Harper & Row, New York, NY. 1987. Henderson presents a dozen or more essays by literary writers and poets telling how they took charge of their own careers and published their own work and, often, the works of others as well. Inspiring and reassuring. You really ought to read it.

Kent, Peter. *Poor Richard's WebSite. TopDrawer* Books. Every serious writer needs a website that will present an easily accessible bio, credits, and work samples. Kent tells you how to build yours.

Kremer, John. *1001 Ways to Market Your Books*. Open Horizons. 1998. *1001 Ways* is a great idea-generator. When sales on one of my books are languishing, I browse through Kremer. Almost always, I will discover an avenue I have not explored, or something Kremer says will bring another, related idea to mind. An excellent resource for anyone selling books.

Levin, Martin P. *Be Your Own Literary Agent: The Ultimate, Insider's Guide to Getting Published.* Ten Speed Press. The best book ever written on freelance agreements, book contracts, and the opportunities, perils and pitfalls of doing business as a writer. Highly recommended.

Poynter, Dan. *The Self-Publishing Manual.* Para Publishing. A thorough introduction to the self-publication and marketing of adult nonfiction. Much of the information is also of use to literary publishers.

Rosenborg, Victoria. *ePublishing for Dummies.* IDG Books. Many writers are now packaging their own works as e-books and selling them on the Internet (see Chapter 10). This book tells you how to turn your product into a e-book that you can sell from your website.

Wilson, John. *The Complete Guide to Magazine Article Writing.* Writer's Digest Books. WD books publishes a great many books on the freelance trade, and it has a new one on this subject every year. They keep publishing them so they can sell them. If reading *Get Paid to Write!* has convinced you to give magazine writing a try, the next step along the way is to go down to your bookstore and get your hands on Wilson's book.

*A **Writer's Guide to Copyright**.* Poets & Writers, Inc. It may be hard to believe, but few writers are really familiar with copyright law. This book will tell you what you want (and need) to know.

Magazines and Newsletters

American Bookseller. American Booksellers Association, 860 White Plains Road, Tarrytown, NY 10891; 800-637-0037. Published monthly. Read this one in the library and keep up with bookstore trends, what's selling and what's not, and bookstore needs and problems. Knowing these things will give you some insight into bookstore concerns when you approach them about selling your book or giving a reading.

American Poetry Review. 1721 Walnut Street, Philadelphia, PA 19103. Published bimonthly.

Foreword Magazine. Focuses on the world of independent and small-press publishing. *Foreword* is a good place to send your books for review. The magazine has a controlled circulation of 20,000.

Poets and Writers Magazine. Poets & Writers, Inc., 72 Spring Street, New York, NY 10012. Published bimonthly. The best of all magazines for poets and literary authors. Brilliantly edited. Not only a great read, but useful, too.

Publishers Weekly. PW, as it is called, is the trade magazine of the publishing industry. If you are interested in the business of books, subscribe for a year and try it out. Or go to the PW website: publishersweekly.reviewsnews.com.

The Writer. Kalmbach Publishing Company. Published monthly. An old-timer in the field, now with new editorial direction, the magazine publishes articles on the craft of writing from authors who have risen to prominence in their field.

Writer's Digest. Probably the most widely-read magazine for writers, *Writer's Digest* has something of a split personality, combining useful articles on the craft with large numbers of advertisements for "editorial service" and "poetry contests" that one would do well to check out carefully, since many are scams of one sort or another.

Directories and Guides

American Book Trade Directory. R. R. Bowker, 121 Chanlon Road, New Providence, NJ 07974. Lists of bookstores and retail outlets, along with distributors and wholesalers.

American Library Directory. R. R. Bowker, 121 Chanlon Road, New Providence, NJ 07974. Public and school libraries. Each entry also indicates the monies allotted for new purchases.

Bacon's Publicity Checker. Bacon's, 332 South Michigan Avenue, Chicago, IL 60604. Updated annually.

Bacon's Radio/TV Directory. Bacon's, 332 South Michigan Avenue, Chicago, IL 60604. Updated annually.

Contemporary Authors. Gale Research Inc., P.O. Box 33477, Detroit, MI 48232. You can get listed here, once you have published. Write for the proper form.

Directory of Poetry Publishers. Dustbooks, P.O. Box 100, Paradise, CA 98967; 800-477-6110. This directory lists magazines and publishers who are receptive to poetry and literary manuscripts. These publications come and go with alarming speed, so consult the latest edition for the most current address.

***The Foundation Center**, 79 Fifth Avenue, New York, NY 10003-3050; 212-620-4230. There are regional offices at 1001 Connecticut Avenue, NW, Suite 938, Washington, DC 20036; at 312 Sutter Street, San Francisco, CA 94108; and at 1356 Hanna Building, 1422 Euclid Avenue, Cleveland, OH 44115. Contact the Foundation Center for information on grants for writers.

***Gale Directory of Publications and Broadcast Media**. Edited by Karen E. Koek end Julie Winklepleck. Gale Research Inc, P.O. Box 33477, Detroit, MI 48232. Names and addresses of print and electronic media.

***Gebbie's All-In-One Directory**. Gebbie Press. This is an easy-to-use directory of magazines, newspapers, and radio and TV stations. It is also available as an electronic mailing list. You can get the information you need at www.gebbie.com.

***The International Directory of Little Magazines and Small Presses**. Dustbooks, P.O. Box 100, Paradise, CA 95967; 800-477-6110.

***Literary Market Place**. R. R. Bowker, 121 Chanlon Road, New Providence, NJ 07974. Updated annually. Usually referred to simply as *LMP*, *Literary Market Place* is the most complete directory of all persons and organizations associated with the publishing business: publishing houses and their specialties, editors, agents, book clubs, manufacturers, suppliers, etc. A new edition is published each year. While addresses may not change rapidly, the names of editors do change. Always use the latest issue available to you.

***Literary Bookstores**. An efficient way to locate 275 American bookstores that are hospitable to contemporary fiction and poetry.

***Poet's Market: Where & How to Publish Your Poetry**. Edited by Judson Jerome et al. Writer's Digest Books, 1807 Dana Avenue, Cincinnati, OH 48207. Published yearly.

***Publisher's Directory**. Edited by Thomas M. Bachmann. Gale Research Inc., P.O. Box 33477, Detroit, MI 48232. This resource lists small and specialty publishers.

***Publication Grants for Writers & Publishers**. Oryx Press, 4041 North Central at Indian School Road, Phoenix, AZ 85012-3397. This manual tells you how to write and submit proposals for grants.

Organizations and Networking

It is stimulating to meet others interested in the same things that interest you and exchange ideas, information, and news of opportunities. By attending local meetings or reading the newsletters of national organizations, you will learn about new magazines, new publishers, new foundations, grant opportunities, writers conferences, literary competitions, job opportunities, and more. Networking begins at home.

If you live in New York, Los Angeles, or San Francisco, "local" also means "national." But in every town of any size there guilds, clubs and associations for writers and poets. They offer everything from moral support to publication opportunities and everything in between: conferences, critique groups, workshops and competitions.

In Savannah, Ga., where I now live, there is a very active writing community, but no organization of practicing writers. I am now in the process of forming one.

Before that, I lived in Coral Springs, a suburb of Fort Lauderdale, Florida. Just to the north is the Poets of the Palm Beaches club. In Miami, to the south, is the National Writer's Association, South Florida Chapter. There is the Palm Beach Book Fest in the Spring and the Miami Book Fair in the Fall, both of which draw name novelists, poets, dramatists, and journalists as speakers and as attendees.

In North Carolina, where I spent many years teaching and publishing magazines, there was the statewide North Carolina Writers Network, with its headquarters in the Chapel Hill-Carrboro area, as well as writers' clubs in the towns where I lived.

Look up your local clubs. Membership is usually open to anyone interested in writing and publishing.

Glossary

agent: Person who sells literary products to publishers on behalf of an author.

alley: The white space between the columns on a page.

alignment: Orientation of type with regard to edges of the column or paper, such as aligned right (flush right), aligned left (flush left), and aligned on center (centered).

anecdote: A brief illustration of a point made in an article. An anecdote consists of a general observation, an example, and often a quote.

available for interview form: A form sent to radio and TV stations in order to garner interview opportunities. Contains author information and suggested interview subject matter.

author's alterations: Changes made by and at the sole discretion of the author after initial typesetting is done.

back matter: Appendices, index, author bio, order form and other materials which may or may not be included in the back of a book.

billboard paragraph: Paragraph following the lead that tells the reader what he can expect to find in the article.

bullet: Bold dot often placed before each item in a list to set it off from the other items.

byline: Line following the title that credits the author.

camera ready: Pages of a book or other publication ready for the printer to use to make negatives, plates, or digital files.

capabilities brochure: Brochure presenting the tasks that a company or individual is capable of accomplishing for a client as well as the resources that the company or individual has available.

cataloging-in-publication data: Library of Congress cataloging data usually printed on the copyright page to assist librarians in cataloging a book.

clip art: Drawings available for purchase for unlimited reproduction. Clip art is in the public domain. Clip art collections may be purchased in printed form or on computer disks.

clips: Photocopies of articles that are used for promotional purposes. Well-chosen clips are often enclosed with a query.

column inch: One vertical inch of space in a printed column of type, most often in a newspaper.

consumer magazine: Magazines of the kind normally sold on the racks in bookstores and newsstands.

copyright: Certification of ownership of a work by a writer, photographer, artist or organization. Notice of copyright is normally printed on the back of the title page in books. The line beneath a photograph or other art identifies the person who created it or, in some cases, the publication that gave permission for its use.

copy editor: Person who checks and corrects a manuscript for spelling, grammar, punctuation, inconsistencies, inaccuracies, and conformity to style requirements. Also called line editor. The copy editor is not the same as a proofreader, who checks only for typographical and other mechanical errors.

cutline: The editorial matter placed beside or beneath a photograph which describes the image depicted.

dash: Typographic mark that indicates a break between thoughts. An em dash (—) is longer than an en dash (–), which is longer than a hyphen (-).

desktop publishing: Term invented by Apple Computer in the mid-1980s to describe the revolutionary typesetting and graphic arts capabilities of their new Macintosh computer and laser printer.

dingbat: Typographic symbol used for emphasis or decoration.

drop cap: Large capital letter that extends down into the first two or more lines. Used as a design element.

dummy: A rough approximation of a finished publication, made by drawing it or by actually pasting up finished elements.

ebook: Book formatted to be delivered to the reader electronically and read on a computer screen or other similar device.

editorial matter: All of the textual matter (exclusive of advertising) in a publication. Successful newspapers and many magazines approach a ratio of 30 percent editorial matter to 70 percent advertising.

edition: All the books sharing the same textual content. When you go back to press for additional books, this is called a second printing. If you add or subtract significant material, the new books are called a second edition.

electronic rights: Rights to sell a book through some means of electronic distribution.

fair use: Provision of the copyright law that allows short quotations from a copyrighted product to be used without permission of the copyright holder.

feature article: Newspaper article that reads more like a magazine article than a news article.

filler: Short items used to fill small blank spaces in a layout. Short, humorous verse can be used as filler.

folio: Term used to designate the page number.

font: A typeface family and all its characters and symbols.

footer: Information, such as page number or chapter title, that appears regularly at the bottom of every page; running foot.

format: Trim size or chosen page design of a book.

front matter: All the pages in a book before the text actually begins, consisting of title page, copyright page, table of contents, dedication and other preliminary matter.

galley (galleys): Preliminary proofs of actual pages. "Bound galleys" are often sent out for review before the actual print run of finished copies.

graph: Jargon for "paragraph."

gutter: The white space between two facing pages. See "jump the gutter."

halftone: A black-and-white photograph, as it appears in a printed book.

hard copy: Pages printed out on paper as distinguished from those on disk or transmitted electronically.

house magazine: A company magazine, published for its employees and customers.

imprint: In book publishing, the name of the publisher as it appears on the title page. Some publishing companies have multiple imprints.

ISBN: Abbreviation for "International Standard Book Number." Every book published needs one of these, obtained from the R. R. Bowker Company. When you have an ISBN you will be listed in *Books In Print*, the chief national database of published works.

italic type: Type slanted to the right to resemble handwriting, as distinguished from roman type. *This sentence is set in italic type.*

jumpline: A line beneath a column indicating that the story "jumps" to (is continued on) another page.

jump the gutter: Said of art elements or copy that cross over the white space between two facing pages.

justified type: A column of type is said to be justified when both the left and right margins are even.

kicker: Short phrase, usually placed at the top left of a headline, designed to attract the interest of the reader.

kill fee: A fee paid to a writer by a magazine which declines to publish a contracted-for piece of writing.

lead: First paragraph of an article, designed to capture the reader's attention and interest.

leading: The distance between the baseline of two succeeding lines of type.

line art: Drawings or other art that have no grays or continuous tones.

mark up: Instructions written on a manuscript to let the typographer know the font, size, leading, etc. to use.

masthead: Block of information in a publication that lists publishing, production, and editorial staffs. Gives addresses and telephone numbers for key departments.

media kit: Collection of public relations material gathered by a writer for the use of print or electronic media and for other promotional uses.

mind-map: Technique for enhancing the creation of ideas.

newsprint: Inexpensive paper on which newspapers are printed.

niche market: A relatively narrow market consisting of readers or consumers interested in a specific topic or subject matter.

on spec: An article submitted to an editor without a firm contract is said to have been submitted "on spec."

op-ed page: The page opposite the editorial page in a newspaper, usually containing commentary and opinion. Sometimes open to freelance submissions.

page proof: Proof of type and graphics as they will look on the finished and printed pages, complete with elements such as headings and rules.

paradigm: An established pattern followed for the accomplishment of a task. Chapter 5 describes the "freelancer's paradigm."

payment on acceptance: A fee paid when an article is accepted for publication, as distinguished from a fee paid when an article is published.

perfect bind: Bookbinding method where pages are glued into a paper cover that is squared off on the spine.

pica: A horizontal unit of measurement used in publishing. Column width, for instance, is usually described in picas. There are approximately six picas in an inch.

PMS: Pantone Matching System, used to specify color.

POD (print on demand): A new technology permitting the inexpensive manufacture of limited numbers of books, even one at a time.

point: The unit of measure used to express the size (height) of type and leading. There are 72 points in an inch.

point-of-purchase display: Rack that contains books for display near the cash register.

profile: An article which deals with the personality and career of the person it is written about.

proofread: To read a manuscript to detect errors in typesetting. Proofreading is a skill that many writers, though thoroughly familiar with the rules of grammar and orthography, do not possess.

proofreader's marks: Standard symbols and abbreviations used to correct manuscripts and proofs.

publisher: CEO or owner of a publishing company. If you self-publish, you become the CEO of your own publishing company. Also, the person with overall responsibility for the publication of periodicals or books.

pull quote: Colorful quote from a story set in larger type and placed between rules or emphasized in some other way to attract reader interest. Also known as a "blurb."

round up article: A magazine article which gathers the opinions of various specialists on a given subject.

query: Letter written by a writer to an editor offering an article for sale.

reading fee: A fee sometimes charged by marginal agents to read and report on a writer's submission. Such fees are not sanctioned by the AAR.

saddle stitch: A binding method whereby pages are stapled together on the spine.

sans-serif type: Type without serifs.

serial rights: Rights to publish a piece of writing in a periodical.

serif: A decorative embellishment at the ends of the elements of a type character.

service article: An article which tells the reader how to reach a particular goal or accomplish a particular task.

sidebar: Short segment of information related to the text but set off from it in some way. There are sidebars in this book, shaded in gray and set in a different, contrasting font.

slant: An author's approach to his subject matter. A slant can be polemical, humorous, analytical, intellectual, etc.

subhead: A caption inserted between paragraphs of text. The effect of the subhead is to break up long stretches of editorial matter, drawing the eye of the reader along and enhancing readability.

syndicate: An organization that sells columns, features, and other editorial matter to periodical publishers.

terms and conditions: Specific details of a contract.

tips booklet: Brief booklet listing advice, usually numbered, on how to accomplish something. "101 Ways to Organize Your Office" might be the title of a tips booklet.

trade journal: Magazine intended to be read by the practitioners of a profession or trade.

transition: Words or phrases with which a writer creates logical sequences of ideas and leads a reader through his work. *However, therefore,* and *nevertheless* are transitional words.

typeface: A font is a type family. A typeface refers to any one member of that family.

type family: A group of related typefaces with the same name, such as Times roman, Times italic, Times roman bold, and Times bold italic.

type size: The height of a typeface, measured from the top of the ascenders (i.e., the stem of an "h") to the bottom of the descenders (i.e., the tail of a "g").

type style: Refers to the member of the type family chosen, such as roman (also called plain), italic, or bold.

typography: The art of setting type. Also refers to the look of type on the page.

work made for hire: Ordinarily, creative works are the intellectual property of the creator. However, when explicitly agreed to by contract, the work becomes the intellectual property of the party specified in the contract, usually the person or organization paying for the creation of the work.

writer's block: Sterile period suffered by some writers when the creative juices just don't seem to be flowing.

—Index—

About the Author

Tom Willams has written for magazines ranging from *Esquire* to *Writer's Digest*. The author of fourteen books, Williams is comfortable on both sides of the editorial desk.

His learning curve was one that all writers are familiar with. "I struggled while learning the ropes," he explains, " persevered while breaking in, then prospered as I began to understand what the business of writing was all about. Best of all, I have never in my life had to do anything to make a living that I wouldn't have done for fun anyway. I do love this business."

In 1979, Williams bought *The Mecklenburg Gazette*, a weekly newspaper in North Carolina. Three years later, by the time he sold his paper for what he calls "a nifty profit," he had hands-on knowledge of every step of the publishing process: editing, typesetting, publication design, and photography. "On a weekly newspaper," he says, "you have to do it all." He had also had "a crash course in the economic realities that underlie any publishing venture."

Subsequently, Williams founded Venture Press (now Williams & Company), a book publishing company. The company list includes how-to books and ebooks for writers and publishers, historical reprints, civic histories, folklore, oral history and poetry.

He has started and published many magazines, including *Tar Heel: The Magazine of North Carolina* (a state-wide magazine), *The New East*, *NC East*, and other regional, consumer magazines.

Readers of this book can contact Tom Williams through his website at www.PubMart.Com.

Sentient Publications, LLC, publishes books on cultural creativity, experimental education, transformative spirituality, holistic health, new science, ecology, and other topics, approached from an integral viewpoint.

Our authors are intensely interested in exploring the nature of life from fresh perspectives, addressing life's great questions, and fostering the full expression of the human potential. Sentient Publications' books arise from the spirit of inquiry and the richness of the inherent dialogue between writer and reader.

Our Culture Tools series is designed to give social catalyzers and cultural entrepreneurs the essential information, technology, and inspiration to forge a sustainable, creative, and compassionate world.

We are very interested in hearing from our readers. To direct suggestions or comments to us, or to be added to our mailing list, please contact:

SENTIENT PUBLICATIONS, LLC

1113 Spruce Street

Boulder, CO 80302

303-443-2188

contact@sentientpublications.com

www.sentientpublications.com